The

Year

of the

Poet VI

December 2019

The Poetry Posse

inner child press, ltd.

The Poetry Posse 2019

Gail Weston Shazor

Shareef Abdur Rasheed

Teresa E. Gallion

hülya n. yılmaz

Kimberly Burnham

Tzemin Ition Tsai

Elizabeth Esguerra Castillo

Jackie Davis Allen

Joe Paire

Caroline 'Ceri' Nazareno

Ashok K. Bhargava

Alicja Maria Kuberska

Swapna Behera

Albert 'Infinite' Carrasco

Eliza Segiet

William S. Peters, Sr.

General Information

The Year of the Poet VI
December 2019 Edition

The Poetry Posse

1ˢᵗ Edition : 2019

Publisher Information
1ˢᵗ Edition : Inner Child Press
intouch@innerchildpress.com
www.innerchildpress.com

ISBN-13 : 978-1-970020-97-7 (inner child press, ltd.)

$ 12.99

WHAT WOULD
LIFE
BE WITHOUT
A LITTLE
POETRY?

$\mathcal{D}$edication

This Book is dedicated to

Poetry . . .

The Poetry Posse

past, present & future

our Patrons and Readers

the Spirit of our Everlasting Muse

&

the Power of the Pen

to effectuate change!

In the darkness of my life
I heard the music
I danced . . .
and the Light appeared
and I dance

Janet P. Caldwell

Table of Contents

The Poetry Posse

Table of Contents . . . *continued*

December's Featured Poets   111

Inner Child News   147

Other Anthological Works   169

Foreword

Throughout the year, we, the members of the Poetry Posee, have endeavored to introduce you to various parts of the world.

This month's edition of The Year of the Poet, December, is no different. Therefore, we, The Poetry Posee, humbly offer up, in verse, for your enjoyment, for your utmost pleasure some of the sights, sounds, tastes and pleasures that are to be found in Australia.

So, come to the poetic table!

We, the Poetry Posse of 2019 invite you to savor each of our family members' offerings.

Through hungering-searching eyes of education or from desire-thirsting imagination, perhaps they will but serve you as an appetizer? Should that be the case, we humbly invite you, dear reader, to venture out far beyond the table set before you. Choose, for yourself, this day, to sample the delights that creatively satisfy your hunger for that which is Australia.

Jackie Davis Allen
jackiedavisallen.com

World Healing, World Peace Foundation
human beings for humanity

worldhealingworldpeacefoundation.org

World Healing, World Peace 2020
International Poetry Symposium

Dear Friends & Family . . . Poets, Poetry Lovers & Humanitarians

We are so excited at ICPI, Inner Child Press International, as we have begun to mobilize for the upcoming epic event of the 'World Healing, World Peace 2020 Poetry Symposium'. Our plans are set for April of 2020. This event will be held in Atlantic City, New Jersey.

We are now collecting names, emails and telephone numbers for all potential resources that can make this event a highly successful, and one of significance that will have a resounding effect on our world and humanity at large. We are also looking for volunteers who can assist us in many areas of facilitation in the planning, staging and execution phases. Going forward, we will be speaking with the business, government, foundation and the private sectors for funding, sponsorship and suitable venues. So, if you know anything, or know someone, we welcome your input and insights.

We will begin shortly to put together our international guest list.

Communicate with us via our email at :

worldhealingworldpeace@gmail.com

or

whwpfoundation@gmail.com

Visit the Web Site(s) :

worldhealingworldpeacepoetry.com

worldhealingworldpeacefoundation.org

World Healing, World Peace 2020 Anthology is now open for submissions.

Submit to :

worldhealingworldpeace@gmail.com

Please share this information

Thank You

Inner Child Press International
'building bridges of cultural understanding'

www.innerchildpress.com

Preface

Yes I am excited and feel accomplished as we close out our sixth year of publishing what I and many others deem to be a worthy enterprise, *The Year of the Poet.*

This past year we have aligned our vision with that of UNESCO as it honors and acknowledges a variety of Global Indigenous cultures. We are now moving forward to our seventh year of publishing. For 2020, we will be focused on acknowledging and poetically sharing our insights on the theme of Nobel Peace Prize recipients. Hopefully thorugh our sharing each month, our poetry can have a profound effect on our global consciousness and the need for peace while educating ourselves and our readership about some of the individuals who have made history through their efforts to promulgate peace for all of humanity.. We are on our way to hitting yet another milestone. Needless to say, I am elated.

To reiterate, our initial vision was to just perform at this level for the year of 2014. Since that time we have had the blessed opportunity to include many other wonderful poets, word artists and storytellers in the Poetry Posse from lands, cultures and persuasions all over the world. We have featured hundreds of additional poets, thereby introducing their poetic offerings to our vast global audience.

In keeping with our effort and vision to expand the awareness of poets from all walks by making this offerings accessible, we at Inner Child Press International will continue to make every volume a FREE Download. The books are also available for purchase at the affordable cost of $7.00 per volume.

In the previous years, our monthly themes were Flowers, Birds, Gemstones, Trees and Past Cultures. This coming year we have elected to continue our focus of choosing what we consider a significant subject . . . PEACE! In each month's volume you will have the opportunity to not only read at least one poem themed by our Poetry Posse members about such celebrated Peace Ambassadors, but we have included a few words about each individual in our prologue. We hope you find the poetic offerings insightful as we use our poetic form to relay to you what we too have learned through our research in making our offering available to you, our readership.

In closing, we would like to thank you for being an integral part of our amazing journey.

Enjoy our amazing featured poets . . . they are amazing!

Building Cultural Bridges of Understanding . . .

Bless Up . . . From the home in our hearts to yours

Bill

The Poetry Posse
Inner Child Press Ineternational

PS

Do Not forget about the World Healing, World Peace Poetry effort.

Available here

www.worldhealingworldpeacepoetry.com

**For Free Downloads of Previous Issues of
The Year of the Poet**

www.innerchildpress.com/the-year-of-the-poet

poetry is . . . .

Oceania

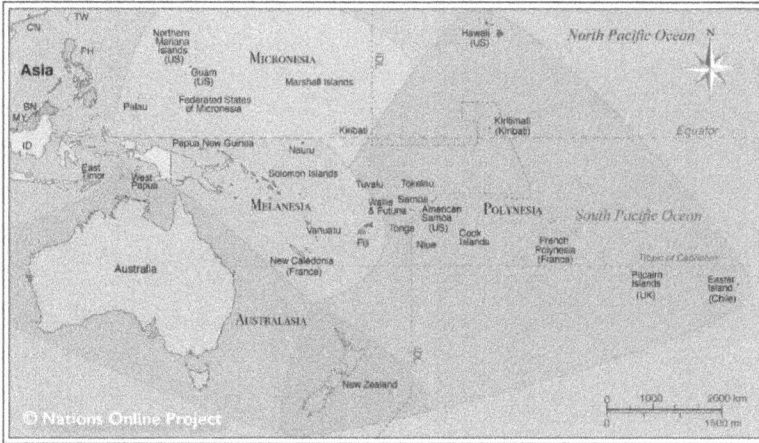

Oceania is a region of the Southern Pacific Ocean that encompasses in excess of three million square miles. This exceptionally expansive region of our world includes Australasia, Melanesia, Micronesia and Polynesia. Oceania spans the eastern and the western hemisphere and has a diverse cultural population of about forty two million people.

For more information about Oceania visit :

https://en.wikipedia.org/wiki/Oceania

Poets . . .
sowing seeds in the
Conscious Garden of Life,
that those who have yet to come
may enjoy the Flowers.

Poets, Writers . . . know that we are the enchanting magicians that nourishes the seeds of dreams and thoughts . . . it is our words that entice the hearts and minds of others to believe there is something grand about the possibilities that life has to offer and our words tease it forth into action . . . for you are the Poet, the Writer to whom the Gift of Words has been entrusted . . .

~ wsp

Coming
April 2020

The
World Healing, World Peace
International Poetry Symposium

Stay Tuned

for more information

intouch@innerchildpress.com

'building bridges of cultural understanding'

www.innerchildpress.com

Poetry succeeds where instruction fails.

~ wsp

I FLY

because ...said the Dreamer to the world. I Can

www.iamjustbill.com

Gail
Weston
Shazor

Gail Weston Shazor

This is a creative promise ~ my pen will speak to and for the world. Enamored with letters and respectful of their power, I have been writing for most of my life. A mother, daughter, sister and grandmother I give what I have been given, greatfilledly.

Author of . . .

"An Overstanding of an Imperfect Love"
&
Notes from the Blue Roof

Lies My Grandfathers Told Me

available at Inner Child Press.

www.facebook.com/gailwestonshazor
www.innerchildpress.com/gail-weston-shazor
navypoet1@gmail.com

Antipodes

My

Feet are

Always near

The equator

Trying to find purchase

And the warmth from your feet

My fingers reach around suns

Nails painted in brilliant oranges

For sometimes my light needs to shine bright

If it is up over or down under

Daybreak

I would kiss you
Small
Gentle, petal soft breaths
Brushing across your
Skin
In moments too slight
To count
Measured pleasures
Leaving sighs
In short trails
I would kiss you
New
At first light
Before the day has its way
And the hunger
For deep, large caresses
Is the only salve that
Covers
I would give you
Small
And the newness
Of me
Before the dawn

Love Poems

I should be writing
Love poems
But the words are stuck
In my jaw
And they taste foreign
In the daylight
So they remain pillow songs
In the vibrato
Of my pulse and resting lids
I dream of your smile
And the way
Your hands feel in the small of my back
I wrap my breath across your shoulders
Whenever you are near
Although the brevity of the moment
Is short of the longing
For abandoned kisses
Drawn long and intimate and
Warmed by the sunlight
You lean into me and
I silently acknowledge the offering
Wishing for time to still
So that your closed eye gift
Will imprint on my bones
Filling the hollow spaces
Even as the rougher touches
Evoke damp memories
I discard the syllables
That seem wholly inadequate
A description of how

Being in your presence
Draws the ink into my lips
But I don't understand
Why. It doesn't find the parchment
I would be writing
Love poems
If only I knew that you wanted them.

Gail Weston Shazor

Alicja
Maria
Kuberska

Alicja Maria Kuberska – awarded Polish poetess, novelist, journalist, editor. She was born in 1960, in Świebodzin, Poland. She now lives in Inowrocław, Poland.
In 2011 she published her first volume of poems entitled: "The Glass Reality". Her second volume "Analysis of Feelings", was published in 2012. The third collection "Moments" was published in English in 2014, both in Poland and in the USA. In 2014, she also published the novel - "Virtual roses" and volume of poems "On the border of dream". Next year her volume entitled "Girl in the Mirror" was published in the UK and "Love me" , " (Not)my poem" in the USA. In 2015 she also edited anthology entitled "The Other Side of the Screen".

In 2016 she edited two volumes: "Taste of Love" (USA), "Thief of Dreams" (Poland) and international anthology entitled " Love is like Air" (USA). In 2017 she published volume entitled "View from the window" (Poland). She also edits series of anthologies entitled "Metaphor of Contemporary" (Poland)

Her poems have been published in numerous anthologies and magazines in Poland, the USA, the UK, Albania, Belgium, Chile, Spain, Israel, Canada, India, Italy, Uzbekistan, Czech Republic, South Korea and Australia. She was a featured poet of New Mirage Journal (USA) in the summer of 2011.

Alicja Kuberska is a member of the Polish Writers Associations in Warsaw, Poland and IWA Bogdani, Albania. She is also a member of directors' board of Soflay Literature Foundation.

Australia - the land of dreams

On the sandy soil, the wind makes a symbol of eternity.
It leads along the dreamy path marked out by ancestors.
The right direction is indicated by the Uluru monolith.

Churing remained after the past generations of sleep time.
Oval stones are hidden in the holy places of *oknanikilla*
There, as in rock cocoons, souls sleep until they are born
again.

Time carries death and life like a boomerang.
Before the next revival - a long and stone sleep awaits.
Ritual songs and dances wake the dead to a new life.

Heart of the House

I take a small surface,
intercede solid lock for the doors
and say with pride " it is my new home"

I live there a few years.
Walls absorb sounds and thoughts,
small fortress guards privacy.

Memories settle as dust on the shelves
- some favorite books,
trinkets from the distant journeys

I buy or throw away items.
Dresses in the closet change fashions
but I still say "my home"

I move out
and give my keys to the other people.
Silence says goodbye indifferently.

My Old House

I know well all metamorphosis of this house.
The new aesthetics
took off its rich ornaments,
The renovations
deprived the subtle beauty of Art Deco.
Entangled by grapes,
it lies dormant for years
in the shadow of lindens .

Stone stairs buckled
under the weight of many feet.
After the rain, in the mirror of a puddle,
the sky is reflected
Brass door handle,
in the shape of a dragon ,guards happiness
and the oak door
defends admission of the foreigners.

I sometimes dream of my happy childhood,
wander along corridors and elegant lounges,
visit the attic filled with memories.
I listen to the rustling of fans and dresses with bustle.

Not so long ago the age of refined ladies passed.
The distant relatives smile from the old photographs.
 I walk along a thin thread woven by time.
I have a key to non-existent door .

Jackie Davis Allen

Jackie Davis Allen

Jackie Davis Allen, otherwise known as Jacqueline D. Allen or Jackie Allen, grew up in the Cumberland Mountains of Appalachia. As the next eldest daughter of a coal miner father and a stay at home mother, she was the first in her family to attend and graduate from college. Her siblings, in their own right, are accomplished, though she is the only one, to date, that has discovered the gift of writing.

Graduating from Radford University, with a Bachelors of Science degree in Early Education, she taught in both public and private schools. For over a decade she taught private art classes to children both in her home and at a local Art and Framing Shop where she also sold her original soft sculptured Victorian dolls and original christening gowns.

She resides in northern Virginia with her husband, taking much needed get-aways to their mountain home near the Blue Ridge Mountains, a place that evokes memories of days spent growing up in the Appalachian Mountains.

A lover of hats, she has worn many. Following marriage to her college sweetheart, and as wife, mother, grandmother, teacher, tutor, artist, writer, poet and crafter, she is a lover of art and antiques, surrounding herself, always, with books, seeking to learn more.

In 2015 she authored *Looking for Rainbows, Poetry, Prose and Art*, and in 2017, *Dark Side of the Moon*. Both books of mostly narrative poetry were published by Inner Child Press and were edited by hulya n. yilmaz.

in 2019, No Illusions.Through the Looking Glass, which was nominated to be considered for a Pulitzer Prize by the publisher and editor of InnerChild Press, ltd.

http://www.innerchildpress.com/jackie-davis-allen.php
jackiedavisallen.com

Australia: A Sovereign Country

Listen! Sydney! Hear the operatic voices!
Ah, Melbourne, she is a feast for the eyes.
Visit her museums, exclaim over her art.
Tour Australia, her landscape,
Islands, numerous large and small.

The Great Barrier Reef, rainforests. Oh my!
Pleasures, treasures, above, below the sky,
Australia is a surfer's paradise!
The Gold Coast awaits as the Commonwealth
Of Australia beckons. Savor her night skies.

So pack your bags, bring your pen and pad.
Off to Perth! Go with laptop and camera, too!
Despite being the smallest continent,
Australia is the largest country on earth.
Avail yourself of her natural wonders!

Beaches, deserts, the Outback, the bush,
Tasmania. Hush! The death toll rises.
Bushfires inflame the land and protestors' anger.
Should the opportunity arise, go, visit
The mainland. Or Australia's many islands.

Me, at Eighty-three

Today as in bed I lie, no longer
Nimble nor so spry, I replay some scenes
From all of my yesterdays. Despite the springs
Curling up and railing against the clock,
I am still the same old me.

I am and have always been my own person.
I am the sum total of all that I have seen,
And done. And have yet to see or do.

In my growing up years,
A child of a stay-at-home Mom
And a coal-mining Dad, I wore shoes
With slits cut in the toes. I had to wait
For new shoes, come September, to wear to school.

I was naive long before I ever knew
That going barefoot was something for which
Outsiders thought I should be ashamed.

Regardless of shoes, purchased or not,
My mind traveled in giant steps, in and around
The four corners of the house. Much like
A coal-truck, I carried more than capacity's load...
The speed and destination, aside.

Upon occasion, maybe once a month, my parents
Went to town. That is, if Dad's paycheck
Would reach as far after paying some on the bills.

There was always the light bill, the charges
At the B. & L. Maytag, and something
Against the ever mounting I.O.U.

At the store, the one down the road...
The one that held the balance
Of our lives in its hands.

Troubles were a'plenty without wondering
If there was gas enough in the tank. Or, if they,
Or we might be able to pass by, undetected.

It was a one stop shop holding the monopoly
Of their employees' lives, their paychecks and
All that they owed to the company store.
My dreams screamed at night. I still see them
Counting, mourning, the cost in lives.

As next to the eldest, I stood watch. Stayed behind
With the little ones. My siblings, many in number.
Their names lost, so too those of the hollers.

Memory wanes on the way to the county seat.
It is a time that has mostly escaped me.
I don't know why. I traveled not far from home,
Walking the mile or two's distance to school.
Or maybe, I rode a bus?

Perhaps it was Virginia. Maybe?
Near the coal fields? West Virginia?
Wherever it was, the house stood on stilts.

A labor of love, stick-built, its back brushed
Up against the foot of the mangled hill.
Not unlike the backs of all the menfolk.
It was a long time ago. So, if you please,
You'll pardon me?
I can't say for sure,
But I think it was built by my father

And some of his brothers.
It was a long time ago.
A very long time ago.

Once my fingers played my song,
Tapping out its tune
Against my prayers, my dreams.

Now, I am left wondering about the time
Of reckoning, my pillow wet with pain
And stained with tears.
Yet it finds me cherishing
What I can't explain.

A cold and hard winter warning
Has too long beat its wet
And hard path over the tin roof of my youth.

My recollections, my life's intent,
My vitality spent. Even still,
At the age of eighty-three
I love to sing its song.
I love to hear its music.

Mostly, But Not All, Forgotten

Shelling peas, sitting out on the porch,
A tea towel covers ample, their laps.
Thick ankles peek out from beneath
1950s hemmed dresses, fourteen inches
Measured up from the pine board floor.

The 1950s pale-painted green-glider
Creaks from the weight of time.
Pauses for but a moment,
While flies caught in yellow sticky
Tape dot their funeral ribbons:
The coffin strips, the death scene
Hangs from the blue board ceiling.

The road oozes black, hot and sticky.
Like the day, the air is stagnated, sickly.
The color of coal is like the N &W cars
Across the way, waiting for the engine
Its steam power, silent, as if it has died.

Hanging over our heads, the thought:
Eventually there will come a time
When all is washed clean. Pray then
For rain, a thunderstorm to hide
Tears stifled, held back with iron of will.

Softened by white lightening swigs
That lighten the loads of men and women folk,
Gossiping, gasping, political correctness
Holds to heaving breast, tight clutching fears.
Too near to the side of the framed board house
Uniformed men alight, dispatched with guns,
Others exiting from backs of state-owned vehicles.

Toting weapons, back and forth, sun glasses
Dark with warning impact, authority,
Reflect images, men, zebra-like animals;
Their stripes black and white, with chains
Around black faces' weary ankles, balls, too.

Unable to roll, to escape, but on whites,
Badges shine silver-like with mores' authority.
Grim, ash-white faces stand with determination
Vigilant, ever at the ready, guarding captive
Dark faces, innocently painted by birth's brush.

No choice in the currency, then, or today
Yet for some reason they must now pay.
But, why, oh, why must they struggle
Like in a side show, while, we, Momma
Auntie, Maw-Maw and little old me, who
In winters be white as light bread?

Yet with summer's sun,
We darken naturally while down by the road,
The striped uniforms bow their heads
And I cowering, begin to bawl.
This ain't no movie!

It is a world of comprehension, or not
Depending upon where one sits or stands
And back in the mountains, white and quiet,
We lesser captives of the times, thought ourselves
Hostages, held by the urgency of coal's black lungs.

What a shock, reality of the world revealed!
Despite lack of radio, television, and magazines,
Steel rimmed sunglasses bore holes
Into young psyches with the somberness
Of a truth, the likes of which I hadn't known existed.

Most of those actors, those players,
Are now silent, dead and gone.
The script, its history, like a bad play
Has been mostly forgotten.
But not entirely.

Tzemin Ition Tsai

Dr. Tzemin Ition Tsai (蔡澤民博士) was born in Republic of China, in 1957. He holds a Ph.D. in Chemical Engineering and two Masters of Science in Applied Mathematics and Chemical Engineering. He is a professor at Asia University (Taiwan), editor of "Reading, Writing and Teaching" academic text. He also writes the long-term columns for Chinese Language Monthly in Taiwan.

He is a scholar with a wide range of expertise, while maintaining a common and positive interest in science, engineering and literature member. He is also an editor of "Reading, Writing and Teaching" academic text and a columnist for *'Chinese Language Monthly'* in Taiwan

He has won many national literary awards. His literary works have been anthologized and published in books, journals, and newspapers in more than 40 countries and have been translated into more than a dozen languages.

An Unexpected Glimpse of a Passing Beauty

My old yellow dog
Accompanied me into the depths of the forest buried in the
mountain bay
As usual
Just relying on that 24 dorsal bones to take on the big
responsibility
Carrying my old canvas bag obliquely over my shoulders
A small camera
A sketchbook
A box of different kinds of pencils
Two pieces of steamed bread
Firmly put down my feet
Totally did not expect to
At the end of the creek, the spring suddenly drilled into the
ground
The misty fog caused the inexplicable melancholy to
continue my original dream

No inns can be found in this mysterious mountain bay
Only to find a steady rock for resting in the shade of the
tree
Facing the creek, I sat cross-legged
Grasses and trees were all coming to wave their hands
A screaming scream caused a short silence around
I looked around
It was on the branch without lights or fires
An unexpected glimpse
I didn't read or write, just drew the five-color fluster bird
with my paper and strokes
Waiting

It spread its wings
And disappear like the wind
Let the song that have been brewing in my chest for a long
time
Be melancholy sung

The Songs Always Weeping as the Sun is Going Down

Time always seems rushed and precise.
I couldn't help but watch the sun go down the mountain.
Like this highland,
Towering into the sky along the edge of the sea.
What kind of sound of nature will forget all of the warnings.
Mother was gradually drifting away
Yes, she will does eventually leave.
The song that should sound when the sun sets.
Keep silent.

Wind blowing over the farm.
Did not stop playing.
Why did I only hear the sound of the treetops?
Scratching my heart
Scratching my innermost being
Never asked me about the scars left behind
When to fix?
Naturally, you won't ask.
Facing a delicate and frail girl like me.

A loving marriage,
Why was it so unbearable and fragile?
Tribulation of war, lingering shadow of death,
Forced to take everything away.
Why was everything so pale in my dreams?
But everything in everything,
the very thought of
That kiss has never been realized.
Until the last time we met.

Caged Bird

The wind bear down on me from behind
Mixed with the sounds of the wings
Don't need to care too much
That's not from my wings
Not from my companions too

The wind bypassed the wires and passed through the cage
Did not stop at all
It's me shouted at her
It's me handed over her the words of heart
But forgot
left words to her
Who should the message be handed over to?

Retreated to the nest in the cage
Dodged
The blames from the entire of companions
But unable to resolve the imprisonment in my heart
Also couldn't face the gradually dying wing
I really wanted to sneak a peek
Who was fanning away from the wind?
Who was following the wind that is flying freely?

Tzemin Ition Tsai

Shareef
Abdur
Rasheed

Shareef Abdur Rasheed

Shareef Abdur-Rasheed, AKA Zakir Flo was born and raised in Brooklyn, New York. His education includes Brooklyn College, Suffolk County Community College and Makkah, Saudi Arabia. He is a Veteran of the Viet Nam era, where in 1969 he reverted to his now reverently embraced Islamic Faith. He is very active in the Islamic community and beyond with his teachings, activism and his humanity.

Shareef's spiritual expression comes through the persona of "Zakir Flo" . Zakir is Arabic for "To remind". Never silent, Shareef Abdur-Rasheed is always dropping science, love, consciousness and signs of the time in rhyme.

Shareef is the Patriarch of the Abdur-Rasheed Family with 9 Children (6 Sons and 3 Daughters) and 41 Grandchildren (24 Boys and 17 Girls).

For more information about Shareef, visit his personal FaceBook Page at :

https://www.facebook.com/shareef.abdurrasheed1
https://zakirflo.wordpress.com

Unlike

----

other regions
Oceania encompasses
over 3 million sq. miles
for those who don't know
42 million call it home
34 languages spoken
15 countries make up in
Asia pacific
dominated by smallest
continent Australia,
first occupied indigenous
over 70 thousand years ago
migrated Africa to Asia
unique environment mix
produce rare species
plants, animals
other varieties of life
stretching from southeast Asia
to Hawaii
continental islands
Australia, New Zealand, New
Guinea
Polynesia, Melanesia, Micronesia
Oceania unique, diverse, array of
living beauty

food4thought = education

F4T

Millions of minds solve nothing combined
no matter how smart
if their hearts are dark

observe all the verbs, nouns, pronouns
coming from so called leaders world round
amount to spit on the ground
when no change for the better abounds

BS seems to be the beat to which the world
taps their feet

no matter which news old or new
it's all old

that's how the narrative goes
that's how the current flows

only the maker knows!

mankind is lost
as long as they don't rely on the source
that gave life, death and raises up again
mankind will fall short
if that source they don't exclusively depend

they can't see that ignorance, fleshly desire
rebellion, greed obscures the vision they need
to obtain the best in this life and the next
avoid the eternal black flame fire
and only with mercy allowed to past the test

so, what lasting value does the world contain
to make it worth the wrath, pain
of the eternal black flame?

pray for..,
----
shifa..,
(cure)
to cover me
as i suffer
imprisoned in pain
reminded of frailties
humans plagued
humans beg
for relief
pain speaks
in tongues
harsh tones
deal with this it said
" you can't ignore me "
so i pray, supplicate
for chains to break
comfort me with ease
a break from difficulty
rescue from frailty
just a human being
in need of mercy
won't complain
in pain
faith remains
believe, receive relief
creator speaks
"and when i'm ill it is
he "(Allah) who cures me "
Qur'an: 26,80
rehearse the verse

food4thought = education

Kimberly Burnham

A brain health expert with a PhD in Integrative Medicine, Kimberly Burnham has lived in tropical Colombia; in Belgium during the Vietnam War; in Japan teaching businessmen English; in diverse international Toronto, Canada and several places in the US. Now, she's in Spokane, WA with her wife, Elizabeth, two sets of twins (age 11 & 14) and three dogs. Her recent book, *Awakenings: Peace Dictionary, Language and the Mind, a Daily Brain Health Program* includes the word for peace in hundreds of languages. Kim's poetry weaves through 70 volumes of *The Year of the Poet*, *Inspired by Gandhi*, *Women Building the World*, *A Woman's Place in the Dictionary*, Tiferet Journal, Human/Kind Journal and more.

https://www.nervewhisperer.solutions/
https://www.linkedin.com/in/kimberlyburnham/

Peaceful Listening

Madura a peaceful Indonesian island

means "paradise" in Tamil

we don't hear too much about her

perhaps because "anteŋ" the word for peace

in Madurese also means still, calm, gentle

and most of all quiet

not speaking much

giving more time to listen

to the waves and waterfalls

the wild Banteng and Balinese cattle

and occasionally a wandering whistling duck

Shirt of Peace

Words are amazing
a few letters carry so much meaning
unique in different languages
even in the same language

In Mengen
an Austronesian language of New Britain in Oceania
'Malo" is peace
as well as
a cloth or bark wrapping like a shirt
the shirt of a man
the shirt of a tree
compared in four letters

"Malo" also to become quiet
calm and be at peace
"Ka malo!" is to tell someone
to be quiet
listen and "malolo" means ruins

I wonder at these letters carrying meaning
the inner peace of knowing you are love
that someone would give you the shirt off their back
quietly even when your life feels like it is in ruins

Maaropo Calm

Words describe actions
building an image of a life
on the Oceanic island of Vanuatu
in Mele "maaropo" describes
what a fire does when it burns low
stream subsiding
or when the swelling goes down
and the wind dies
as the sea calms
flattening after a storm

"Tam̃ateemanu" is quietness
while "manumanu" describes a person
a hostage exchanged between villages
to ensure peace "tam̃ate"
calm of the sea and a ceremony
to commemorate peace between tribes
or honor the death of a chief

"Marie" is good
a common greeting "kor ragonaji marie?"
do you feel well?
as "oina" describes the tide when moderately low,
especially in the morning calm
and "sale-jiijiro" is to drift along in calm waters
looking down for fish

Elizabeth E. Castillo

Elizabeth Esguerra Castillo

Elizabeth Esguerra Castillo is a multi-awarded and an Internationally-Published Contemporary Author/Poet and a Professional Writer / Creative Writer / Feature Writer / Journalist / Travel Writer from the Philippines. She has 2 published books, "Seasons of Emotions" (UK) and "Inner Reflections of the Muse", (USA). Elizabeth is also a co-author to more than 60 international anthologies in the USA, Canada, UK, Romania, India. She is a Contributing Editor of Inner Child Magazine, USA and an Advisory Board Member of Reflection Magazine, an international literary magazine. She is a member of the American Authors Association (AAA) and PEN International.

Web links:

Facebook Fan Page

https://free.facebook.com/ElizabethEsguerraCastillo

Google Plus

https://plus.google.com/u/0/+ElizabethCastillo

The Melas Nesoi

The hunter-gatherer people
A culture, oh, so unique
Amidst the tropical rainforests
Their most-cherished habitat.

Melanesians-
Believed in a supernatural force
The "Mana"-
Eclectic people, forgotten not.

We Are Infinite

When I'm missing you

I simply look up

Islands apart,

The thought

That we're looking

At the same sky

Marveling at the same moon,

Settles my anxious heart...

Yes, our mystic connection

Is timeless and infinite

Magically weaved, the Universe

As our Witness

There is simply no End...

Silence

For two hearts that understand each other,

Silence speaks a thousand words

Though unspoken, the connection lives on,

Souls waiting to touch each other

In the physical plane

While apart,

The mind wanders to where you are-

Keeping this promise I kept from the start.

Joe
Paire

Joe Paire

Joseph L Paire' aka Joe DaVerbal Minddancer . . .
is a quiet man, born in a time where civil liberties
were a walk on thin ice. He's been a victim of his
own shyness often sidelined in his own quest for
love. He became the observer, charting life's path.
Taking note of the why, people do what they do. His
writings oft times strike a cord with the
dormant strings of the reader. His pen the rosined
bow drawn across the mind. He comes full-frontal
or in the subtlest way, always expressing in a way
that stimulate the senses.

www.facebook.com/joe.minddancer

What Is This Place

Who are these people that look like me
I wonder in this land down under are they free?
Have the chains of persecution lessoned the populous?
Has their skin fenced them in the land they love?

Aboriginal people, have the original people thinking
We are connected in kind with the land
we are rejected in the eyes of some men
What is this place?

I see strange looking animals and beautiful beaches
I see a mirage as I thirst in desert heat
I see old bones that never made it home
I hear the tone of a didgeridoo

That sound, that sound, that beautiful sound
every shore bare echoes of waves
ancient rock art etched in caves
Australia-Oceana long live pass graves

Travel Woes

I want to travel to North America and speak to the natives
I'm embarrassed now
I want to travel to South America, Mesoamerica
I'm ashamed now
I want to explore the Caribbean, Central and West Africa
Where ever what have you I want to experience the world
I feel I can't now, there's a cloud over my pride
I've traveled before to foreign shores
in uniform and civilian attire
but there's a climate here in which I fear
it's not safe to travel anymore

Hey Joe, hey Joe, such a common name
to get me to purchase what the natives are displaying
This country I love and served in war for,
Now has a reputation, we can't keep our word, LORD!
I want to travel the Middle East, North and South Africa
I want to cruise down the Nile I'd love to visit China,
their cultures so rich but let me remind you
I have travel woes, will I be spit on or dodge thrown stones
my democracies polices has opened up atrocities
We were once the model, so what's truly stopping me
Pride! It's been shattered

Life In General

How often I've wondered about my purpose for living
is there such a thing as a poor philanthropist?
A starving artist,
I think not, although I do hunger for knowledge
life being my college I've learned a lot
how I apply it now follows me
Rhyme and meter double entendre
I speak silent in conversation don't say I didn't warn you
the lucky ones know what they were born to do
I've yet to find out, yet I continue plodding through
What do I want to do, some say I have talent
I'm funny, intelligent but I wonder truly wonder
has my life become relevant, will I be missed?
Will my demise cause weeping eyes
is life simply being born, live and die
Are we no more than a life cycle
buried to be recycled? Life puzzles me
Are we no more than eat and sleep.

hülya
n.
yılmaz

Liberal Arts Emerita, hülya n. yılmaz is a published author, literary translator, and Co-Chair and Director of Editing Services at Inner Child Press International. Her poetic work appeared in an excess of eighty-five anthologies of global endeavors and has been presented at numerous national and international poetry events. In 2018, the Writer's International Network of British Colombia, Canada honored yılmaz with a literary award. As of 2017, two of her poems remain permanently installed in *Telepoem Booth* – a U.S.-wide poetic art exhibition. hülya finds it vital for everyone to understand a deeper sense of self, and writes creatively to attain a comprehensive awareness for and development of our humanity.

Writing Web Site
https://hulyanyilmaz.com/

Editing Web Site
https://hulyasfreelancing.com

oh, woe be upon the nations of Oceania!

1789
William Bligh
an escapee of the Royal Navy
of the United Kingdom, that is
Pitcairn Islands, a British colony
merely one among the too many

the 19th century,
a time of colonial blossoming
Niue, the last island to colonialize
the British are at it anew

the French, the Spanish, the Dutch,
the Germans, the Americans, the Japanese,
each partaking in the bounties as well
insatiable egos had long ago started to swell
native abundance flowered forcefully
under the rulers' prolonged evil spell
the iron fists of all the powers-that-be
frivolously opted for a fatal decree

underground nuclear testing ensued,
the 20th century showed the natives
catastrophes of cruelest absurdity
the United Kingdom and France once more

as for "Mike", world's first hydrogen bomb,
that one was the pride and joy
of the United States

protests fell on deaf ears
yet once again
and again

oh, woe be upon the nations of Oceania!
The so-called civilizations invaded them,
leaving them in dire despair

irony?
the same control-greedy,
very much alive today,
claim preposterously
that they have the last say

oh, woe be upon the nations of this day!
the ruthlessness of old and young colonizers
is eager and determined to be at play

when a HAIKU lacks its title

utter destruction
many sleepers take a side
the heart must decide

hülya n. yılmaz

when a HAIKU lacks its title

utter destruction
many sleepers take a side
the heart must decide

a new day dawned again

inhaling, exhaling in the comfort of a home
running water, heat, food and body intact
luxuries for far too many on Earth
their sufferings . . . oh, they do impact!

knots in the throat, tears in the heart
while sitting on the privileged throne
knowing that there is much good to unearth
and needing to reach out with a helping hand
oh, the soul pains severely
over the aches of the known
and the still-unknown

yet she goes on to remain inside her frame
and devours her by now-cold coffee
one sip at a time, carefree . . .

hülya n. yılmaz

Teresa E. Gallion

Teresa E. Gallion

Teresa E. Gallion was born in Shreveport, Louisiana and moved to Illinois at the age of 15. She completed her undergraduate training at the University of Illinois Chicago and received her master's degree in Psychology from Bowling Green State University in Ohio. She retired from New Mexico state government in 2012.

She moved to New Mexico in 1987. While writing sporadically for many years, in 1998 she started reading her work in the local Albuquerque poetry community. She has been a featured reader at local coffee houses, bookstores, art galleries, museums, libraries, Outpost Performance Space, the Route 66 Festival in 2001 and the State of Oklahoma's Poetry Festival in Cheyenne, Oklahoma in 2004. She occasionally hosts an open mic.

Teresa's work is published in numerous Journals and anthologies. She has two CDs: *On the Wings of the Wind* and *Poems from Chasing Light*. She has published three books: *Walking Sacred Ground, Contemplation in the High Desert* and *Chasing Light.*

Chasing Light was a finalist in the 2013 New Mexico/Arizona Book Awards.

The surreal high desert landscape and her personal spiritual journey influence the writing of this Albuquerque poet. When she is not writing, she is committed to hiking the enchanted landscapes of New Mexico. You may preview her work at

http://bit.ly/1aIVPNq or *http://bit.ly/13IMLGh*

Indigenous Australians

Aboriginal peoples descended from
groups that existed in Australia
and surrounding islands thousands
of years ago.

Archaeological evidence reveals human
remains were present before the advent
of British colonialism.

There is great diversity in different
indigenous communities expressed
in mixture of cultures, customs and
languages.

Reduction of the population occurred
due to diseases such as smallpox and
wars by British settlers against
the first peoples on the continent.

The fact that the aboriginals survive
today is a tribute to courage, strength
and persistence through time of all
indigenous peoples across planet earth.

Salmon

It takes persistence and stamina to swim
against the river to end a life cycle.
In one last defiant act,
lay eggs at the river's bottom
to give yourself relief, sweet death.

Little pearls left behind grow into alvins,
start a new cycle at natures call. They abandon
their birthright, smolt downstream,
grow salt skin, the entry ticket to the sea.

They live life in their own way
until time calls them home
bloated with good news.

A single focused goal powered
by determination and endurance
leads them to swim against the river.

Some will make it.
Some will make an offering to the bears.
Those that reopen the door to home
complete their mating cycle
dropping eggs, joining their ancestors
in sweet death.

Bonding

The open road makes a call.
She cannot resist the nomadic
itch that consumes her.

Metal is pressed below
her foot to cruise down
the highway.

She stops momentarily, drools
over a YouTube landscape
streaming on the computer.

She will just keep to herself
this bond between the video,
the road and her feet.

Ashok K. Bhargava

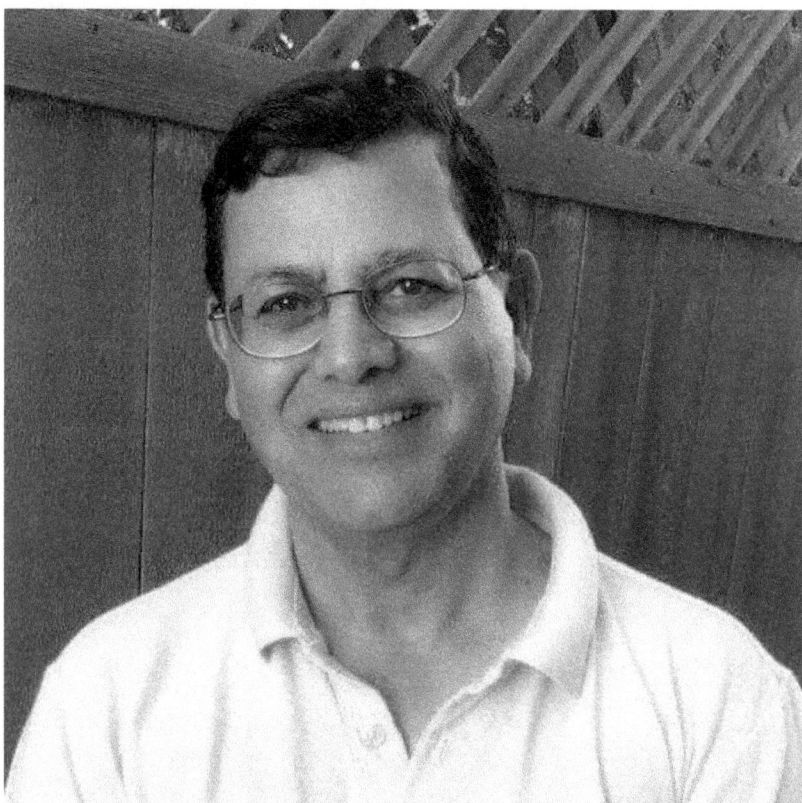

Ashok Bhargava is a poet, writer, community activist, public speaker, management consultant and a keen photographer. Based in Vancouver, he has published several collections of his poems: Riding the Tide, Mirror of Dreams, A Kernel of Truth, Skipping Stones, Half Open Door and Lost in the Morning Calm. His poetry has been published in various literary magazines and anthologies.

Ashok is a Poet Laureate and poet ambassador to Japan, Korea and India. He is founder of WIN: Writers International Network Canada. Its main objective is to inspire, encourage, promote and recognize writers of diverse genres, artists and community leaders. He has received many accolades including Nehru Humanitarian Award for his leadership of Writers International Network Canada, Poets without Borders Peace Award for his journeys across the globe to celebrate peace and to create alliances with poets, and Kalidasa Award for creative writings.

Oceanic Heaven

The seashore at nightfall
is home of the dark waves
until the dawn brings
the orange on the sandy beach.
With a quiver in the morning wind
waves flow backwards
leaving starfish stranded.
The sunrays lay
Sparkling pearls on Oceania.
Flocks of gulls whirl down
In search of food.
Beaches devoid of people
look empty.
It is a lonesome paradise
as it is supposed to be.

Salt Water

a dip in ocean water
didn't absolve
my sins or
primal desires
because
I am
a selfish being
with a lustful
mind
sensuous lips
coveting
heart
dipped in
deceit

rather I
polluted
the pious
waters

Deer Park

break away
from desires
to attain nirvana
echoes all around here

clicking photographs of ruins
of Sarnath
site of Buddha's first sermon
we attempt
in vain
to refute the cravings
of modern bungalows
sculpted lawns
luxury cars
to detach
from the self-made entrapments

Caroline
'Ceri Naz'
Nazareno

Carolin 'Ceri' Nazareno

Caroline 'Ceri Naz' Nazareno-Gabis, World Poetry Canada International Director to Philippines is known as a 'poet of peace and friendship', a multi-awarded poet, editor, journalist, speaker, linguist, educator, peace and women's advocate. She believes that learning other's language and culture is a doorway to wisdom.

Among her poetic belts include 7 th Prize Winner in the 19 th and 20 th Italian Award of Literary Festival; Writers International Network-Canada ''Amazing Poet 2015'', The Frang Bardhi Literary Prize 2014 (Albania), the sair-gazeteci or Poet Journalist Award 2014 (Tuzla, Istanbul, Turkey) and World Poetry Empowered Poet 2013 (Vancouver, Canada). She's a featured member of Association of Women's Rights and Development (AWID), The Poetry Posse, Galaktika Poetike, Asia Pacific Writers and Translators (APWT), Axlepino and Anacbanua.

Her poetry and children's stories have been featured in different anthologies and magazines worldwide.

Links to her works:

panitikan.ph/2018/03/30/caroline-nazareno-gabis
apwriters.org/author/ceri_naz
www.aveviajera.org/nacionesunidasdelasletras/id1181
.html

Blaze of Delight

One, two or more
Waves in the ocean of our lives
In this current time
As it goes back and forth
To remind our worth.

When the luminous hours
Transcend beams of hope
I think of how the stars
Glow more than you'll ever know
Become thrones and tiaras of passion.

Every now and then
To behold a golden cloud
Sometimes the rain of pulse and heartbeat
In thunder and lightning
Cast million of teardrops of joy.

The flower fields in our battlefields
Covered with rhythmic dewdrops
As it sips dazzles of sunlight
Like you and I whispering
The tenderness of our fervent prayers.

The Messenger and The Muse

I am reunited with my bicycle
The happiness is between heaven and earth,
My mind is on a pedestal
For many hours,
I cherish the moment
I found myself—

I am the version of meanings
The trees affirm my presence
Where I throw season's home
Igniting words of wisdom
And carry miracles of growth in every soul
I found my existence.

Sky-life

woman,

become the mosaic

of the crusades you won,

as you aspire to move in calmness

you spring love,

you, the warrior on the edge of time,

will live the star and the sky of LIFE.

Swapna Behera

Swapna Behera

Swapna Behera is a bilingual contemporary poet, author, translator and editor from Odisha, India. She was a teacher from 1984 to 2015. Her stories, poems and articles are widely published in National and International journals, and ezines, and are translated into different national and International languages. She has penned six books. She is the recipient of the Prestigious International Mother Language UGADI AWARD WINNER 2019. She was conferred upon the Prestigious International Poesis Award of Honor at the 2nd Bharat Award for Literature as Jury in 2015, The Enchanting Muse Award in India World Poetree Festival 2017, World Icon of Peace Award in 2017, and the Pentasi B World Fellow Poet in 2017. She is the recipient of Gold Cross of Wisdom Award, the Prolific Poetess Award, The Life time Achievement Award, The Best Planner Award, The Sahitya Shiromani Award, ATAL BIHARI BAJPAYEE AWARD 2018, Ambassador De Literature Award 2018, Global Literature Guardian Award, International Life Time Achievement Award and the Master of Creative Impulse Award. She has received the Honoured Poet of India from the Seychelles Government accredited Literary Society LLSF. Her one poem A NIGHT IN THE REFUGEE CAMP is translated into 50 languages. She is the Ambassador of Humanity by Hafrikan Prince Art World Africa 2018 and an official member of World Nation's Writers Union, Kazakhstan 2018. Italy, the National President for India by Hispanomundial Union of Writers (UHE), Peru, the administrator of several poetic groups, and the Cultural Ambassador for India and south Asia of Inner Child Press U.S.

If you look at the contours

if you look at the contours
seas, hills ,valleys and the pearls
some where the miniscule globe
 snails ,oceans , trees and colours
sing the Anthem to give and live

lo, behold
 mother's milk or the fruits
metaphysically sing ;
a dot in a circle or tune in a soul
the pristine segmentations
certainly create strata of the heritage

if you look at the contours
death and life make the circle
with easy intrusions and dimensions

contours are documents
of dawn and dusk
some written but mostly not yet recorded ....

Salary and Celery

my salary speaks ;
loves, buys ,sings
dances in my purse
twists honeycombs
can bridge the parameters
to paragraphs
 tucked in my pages of life

celery in the garden
gives fragrances to the broth
the greenery oscillates my soul
each morning ....
I smile
end of the month my salary tinkles
 in my pocket or in my account
in the ventilator for my existence
for bread or blankets

the celery smiles in the courtyard
celery and salary march forward
 for the curry in a hurry ....

3 random poems
TERCET

1. The Great Barrier Reef

The Great Barrier Reef
only living organism in belief
can be spotted from space

2. Coral Reefs

coral reefs provide buffer
coasts never suffer
 from waves, storms and floods

3.Oceana

the waves echo ,
to throw the ego
 the rivers merge to search the archipelago ....

TERCET forms are Three lines with the first two rhyming

Albert 'Infinite' Carrasco

Albert "Infinite The Poet" Carrasco is an urban poet, mentor and public speaker.

Albert believes his experience of growing up in poverty, dealing with drugs and witnessing murder over and over were lessons learnt, in order to gain knowledge to teach. Albert's harsh reality and honesty is a powerfully packed punch delivered through rhyme. Infinite grew up in the east part of the Bronx and still resides there, so he knows many young men will follow the same dark path he followed looking for change. The life of crime should never be an option to being poor but it is, very often.

Infinite poetry @lulu.com

Alcarrasco2 on YouTube

Infinite the poet on reverbnation

Infinite Poetry

http://www.lulu.com/us/en/shop/al-infinite-carrasco/infinite-poetry/paperback/product-21040240.html

Australia Oceania

Australasia
Melanesia
Micronesia
Polynesia
Are all in the geographical area of Oceania.
This is the land of many islands,
From aboriginal to modern man.
There's so many wonders on this part of the earth,
Whether you're in Sydney, Melbourne, Brisbane or Perth.
The beaches for swimming and for those that surf.
The outback has kangaroo, wallaby, Tasmanian devils and
koalas
You have Mount Ossa in Tasmania,
And ten deserts including The Simpson and The Great
Victoria,
Tourist come to see all of thee above and the barrier reef in
a huge body of water.
National Parks,
Museums,
Restaurants,
And Art galleries are delightful by courtesy of the Aussies.

Praying for my downfall

They didn't want me to win, they're tired of me shinning so they pray that my light goes dim. I'm on my job writing urban scriptures producing mind blowing pictures of clouds, sunshine and rain as if I was drawing the weather. It's infinite, eight letters, the horizontal eighth number, the way I put words together should make me the eighth wonder of my genre. I went from the streets to stages to published pages, I'm a hustler, there's levels to this, Perico and Manteca were phases, I still have material, it's all mental, ya know memories of the birth circa and trappers at early ages, up to now when most of those trappers or dead or In cages. I got that work. I'm hitting heads like my old environment, I don't have to worry about raids like my old apartments, there's no more wars because of the love for money getting violent and no more lost freedom due to physical confinement. I miss men i bonded with a few years after birth, they say what goes up comes down, so can anyone tell me when are the souls that went to heaven returning to earth?

Lean on me

When dudes was hungry they knew I'll feed em, so they looked for me to eat, when dudes had drama they looked for me because they knew I'll give this cold world some heat, when dudes were making bad moves, I showed them how to navigate these streets. I always wanted for others as I would want for myself, wealth, good health and stealth, ya know get cheddar, stay alive and off the radar.

I learnt the game before I was in the game, I had a head start in hard knocks, I'm talking about spoons to bags, sealed or slabbed rocks, bottle and cans practice shots and how to spot cops trying to infiltrate the block. It takes a village to raise a child, I was an ado out there taking lessons from those living vile, they didn't know they was teaching me, I was just a nosy juvenile.

I didn't look at them as if they were bad, I looked up to them, because where I'm from in the slums I admired those that lived with the "by any means" mentality when chasing that bag. When I got my shot it was as if I was a young money beast released from a cage, I'm was too advanced for youngens, so I was the youngen pushn with older dudes, some twice my age, a few stacks a shift was minimum wage, I put that work in until me and top men was on the same page.

When the top men could no longer stand the heat in the kitchen, got sent up to the yard, found or got sent to god, started smokin or sniffn till they nod, I stood on the trap workin, hustln and stayn alive was my only job. When dudes was hungry they knew I'll be able to feed em, so they looked for me to eat, when nikkas had drama they looked for me because they knew I'll give this cold world some heat, when dudes as making bad moves, I showed them how to navigate these streets. I know the pros and cons, the ying and yang, they joy and pain of the game, it's educational when I speak.

Albert 'Infinite' Carassco

Eliza Segiet

Eliza Segiet - A graduate of Jagiellonian University, The author of poetry volumes. *Romans z sobą* [*Romance with Oneself*] (2013), *Myślne miraże* [*Mental Mirages*](2014), *Chmurność* [*Cloudiness*] (2016), *Magnetyczni* (2018) *Magnetic People*- translation published in The USA in 2018, *Nieparzyści* [*Unpaired*] (2019), A monodrama *Prześwity* [*Clearance*] (2015), a farce *Tandem* [*Tandem*] (2017), Mini novel *Bezgłośni* [*Voiceless*](2019). Her poems can be found in numerous anthologies both in Poland and abroad. She is a member of The Association of Polish Writers and The World Nations Writers Union. The laureate of The International Annual Publication of 2017 for the poem Questions, and for the Sea of Mist in Spillwords Press in 2018. For her volume of Magnetic People she won a literary award of a Golden Rose named after Jaroslaw Zielinski (Poland 2019 r.). Her poem The *Sea of Mists* was chosen as one of the best amidst the hundred best poems of 2018 by International Poetry Press Publication Canada. In The 2019 Poet's Yearbook, as the author of *Sea of Mists*, she was awarded with the prestigious Elite Writer's Status Award as one of the best poets of 2019 (July 2019).

She was awarded *World Poetic Star Award* by World Nations Writers Union – the world's largest Writers' Union from Kazakhstan (August 2019).
In September 2019 she was 1st Place Laureate (Foreign Poetry category) – in Contest *Quando È la Vita ad Invitare* for poem *Be Yourself* (Italy).
Her poem *Order* from volume *Unpaired* was selected as one of the 100 best poems of 2019 in International Poetry Press Publications (Canada).
In November 2019 she is a nominee for Pushcart Prize.

Below the Surface

In the blistering silence,
deedy,
thirsty for gems,
they burrow an uncertain future.
The unrest of the seekers disappears
with
the opalescence of the uncovered stone.

They keep looking

translated by Artur Komoter

- one is not enough.

To fulfill their dreams of wealth,
they settle in the underground
Coober Pedy.

There,
in the desert,
it is better to live below the surface
– the lower the cooler
maybe
– the deeper the closer to the stone prize.
They burrow more corridors of hope
to say
 I have everything. The world can be mine.
Worse, when at the decline of life
they understand that

– no loot
will resurrect lost time.

translated by Artur Komoter

Skies

When the wings fall □
you dive.
You need a moment
to again
rise to the skies.
You have to believe in yourself.
Someone needs to do it first.
Then
others will believe
that you can
also glide.

translated by Artur Komoter

William
S.
Peters Sr.

Bill's writing career spans a period of over 50 years. Being first Published in 1972, Bill has since went on to Author in excess of 50 additional Volumes of Poetry, Short Stories, etc., expressing his thoughts on matters of the Heart, Spirit, Consciousness and Humanity. His primary focus is that of Love, Peace and Understanding!

Bill says . . .

I have always likened Life to that of a Garden. So, for me, Life is simply about the Seeds we Sow and Nourish. All things we "Think and Do", will "Be" Cause and eventually manifest itself to being an "Effect" within our own personal "Existences" and "Experiences" . . . whether it be Fruit, Flowers, Weeds or Barren Landscapes! Bill highly regards the Fruits of his Labor and wishes that everyone would thus go on to plant "Lovely" Seeds on "Good Ground" in their own Gardens of Life!

to connect with Bill, he is all things Inner Child

www.iaminnerchild.com

Personal Web Site

www.iamjustbill.com

Oceania

I tried to swim the seas
Where the oceans run amuck
From grey-tones to azures,
To emerald laden shores

Temperature frigid,
Temperatures warm
And the predator and prey
Swarm, swarm, swarm

The vastness and expanse
As the islands doth enhance
The poetic beauty
Of it all

Can you hear the call?

Memories of sailors searching
For bounty and booty alike . . .
Discovering the unknowns
With a thirst and wonderment
Which has yet to be vanquished

Bibles, guns, whiskey and wooden ships
Coming to conquer
The unspoken tongues

Who will survive who I ask . . .
Yes, who will survive . . .
Oceania ?

I dream of that place

I dream of that place
I once called home,
And there is an acute longing
That pains my heart
When I remember

I have a distant hope
To once again
Feel the soles of my feet
Touch the raw damp earth
In the quiet gardens
Where solace grows
And peace is the yeild
That is borne
Upon every bud and blossom

The trees of this land
Offer a sweet fruit
Of content and smiles
And we, all the children
Were kissed
By gentle breezes and sunshine

Oh, it did rain . . .
Every now and then,
and we all were cleansed
Of our errant thoughts
And our 3rd eye opened
As our brows of sweat . . .
Renewed

There were no lamentations

Yes, I dream,
I dream of that place,
That elusive place
That dances about me
Enticing me and my aspirations
For you,
For the world
For the all of all things

Wonder

I	Just	That	Our	Doing
often	what	have	"here"	"now"
wonder,	are	transcended	are	
	all	before		
	the			
	souls			

We do understand that "energy"
Can not be destroyed,
It just transmutes
To dimensions
We yet to fully comprehend
And therefore yet to . . .
Embrace

It is not the universe
That is expanding,
But that of our . . .
Consciousness

So I ask again
What are they doing
In this moment

This moment in creation
Is as are each and every moment.
It is devoid of time,
For time is the illusion
In which we take stock
Of ourselves

And create our personal esteem
That rests itself on dissolving
Foundations
Of "knowing" . . .

But I ask . . .
What do we know
About tomorrow,
Save our shallow perceptions
Laced with the wisping fabric
Of expectation,
A place where dreams
Become . . .
Necessary

Well . . . there is no more at this time
For me to write,
For I hear
"Wonder"
Whispering my name

December
2019
Featured Poets

~ * ~

Rahim Karim (Karimov)

Sujata Paul

Bharati Nayak

Kapardeli Eftichia

I Fly

because I Can

. . . said the Dreamer to the world.

www.iamjustbill.com

112

Rahim Karim (Karimov)

Rahim Karim (Karimov)

Rahim Karim (Karimov) is an Uzbek-Russian-Kyrgyz poet, writer, publicist, translator. He was born in 1960 in the city of Osh (Kyrgyzstan). Graduate of the Moscow Gorky Literary Institute (1986). Member of the National Union of Writers of the Kyrgyz Republic, member of the Russian Writers' Union, official representative of the International Federation of Russian-Speaking Writers in Kyrgyzstan (London-Budapest), member of the Board of the IFRW, laureate of the Republican Literary Prize named after Moldo Niyaz. The author of the national bestseller "Kamila", the winner of the second prize of the International Book Forum Open Central Asia Book Forum & Literature Festival - 2012 (Great Britain), the nominee for the Russian national literary awards "Poet of the Year 2013", "Poet of the Year 2014", "Writer of the Year 2014", "Poet of the Year 2015","Heritage- 2015", "Heritage-2016", the Prize for them. S. Yesenin (2016). In 2017 he was awarded the silver medal of the Eurasian literary contest LiFFт in the nomination of a Eurasian poet. Co-chairman of the Council of Writers and Readers of the Assembly of Peoples of Eurasia. Author of about 30 books published in Kyrgyzstan, Uzbekistan, Kazakhstan, Ukraine, Belarus, Russia, Great Britain, Canada, Romania, Greece, Netherlands, India, Tunisia, Saudi Arabia, Albania, Belgium, Macedonia, Afghanistan, France, USA etc.

He translated poetry and prose of authors from Kyrgyzstan, Uzbekistan, Russia, Tajikistan, Mongolia, Azerbaijan, Kazakhstan, the Netherlands, Tunisia, Saudi Arabia, Romania, Poland, Macedonia, Croatia, Bosnia and Herzegovina, Iran, Luxembourg etc.

Friendship song

And friendship is an expensive feeling, like love,
Does not like friendship rash steps!
Oh, take care of friendship, good people, -
It is given only as kind as a gift from pearls.

Do not wait in vain from friendship benefits never,
The law of friendship Faith will be forever.
Oh, cherish the friendship, people of the whole Earth,
Treason does not forgive friendship through the year!

Let's sing about the friendship song, together we all sing,
Having put all soul into this song, we will save the world!
We will sing like the sea, coming from distant shores,
Sing like nightingales on branches at night, by day!

She is tender as a rose, friendship, like a flower,
Love water is required at the right time!
She is like a bridge with a hair size
To pass through, he must have honor for the future!

She - the need of the soul, beautiful, good disposition,
War and malice, anger is her sinister enemy!
You will find good friends, if the mind is healthy,
Treason is alien to her, blasphemy and slander!

 Give me a hand, sister, give a hand, stepbrother!
I am not very happy to live in a world without you!
Let's be together on light in the rain, and in hail,
We are passengers of only one ship!

We are rewarded with friendship by the Most High, God,
The faithful motherland is the blue sky.
To glorify friendship every moment is a sacred duty,
She is a sign of purity, take care, people!

It doesn't matter who you are, Uzbek or Uigur
Ukrainian, Tajik, Georgian, Kazakh, Hindu.
Ile Russian, Armenian, Czech, German, Belarusian,
You are first a man, even though you are an Arab, a tungus.

Let's sing about the friendship song, together we all sing,
Having put all soul into this song, we will save the world!
We will sing like the sea, coming from distant shores,
Sing like nightingales on branches at night, by day!

There is no peace, happiness where there is friendship, no
faith,
Life will consist of squabbles, battles, misfortunes.
Do not tarnish your friendship name, banner, honor,
As long as there is Friendship in the world, then Life is!

It doesn't matter who you are, Rahim, Kai, Muhammad,
Ivan, Arthur, Nurtay, Taras, Rome, Salavat.
Michel, Maryam, Arzuu, Barcin Il Karamat,
You are first a man, even though Karl, James, Marat!
Give me a hand, sister, give a hand, stepbrother!
I am not very happy to live in a world without you!
Let's be together on light in the rain, and in hail,
We are passengers of only one ship!

Rahim Karim (Karimov)

My dad is the worst in the world!

I swore again the younger one for the prank, -
I didn't want to cook my own lessons ...
Frowning - offended, a little, a little,
Suddenly he took a notebook and a pen in his hands.

And he wrote the names of all the relatives,
Friends, acquaintances, on a piece of paper - in a cage ...
"Good" - stressed opposite the birdie, -
And in a moment, he circled his marks in red.

Opposite the father's name, however,
Put a cross, he vetoed.
And he wrote beautifully - very clearly:
"My dad is the most, yes, bad in the world!".

No luck with dad son in the world, -
With a bad father lives, alas, oh, have pity!
Let, I did not become an idol for my son,
But I have the best boy in the world!

Disabled people

Rich Planets, just humans,
Do not torment you compassion, pain?
Singing in the markets are songs of the handicapped,
We hurry past to the concert, football !!!

I look into the world again through the window of Khayyam,
-
I only see alms asking.
Hurrying friend, to the wedding, flying,
For the first time you hear their songs with me!

Dressed luxuriously, without offense,
Just look around you.
On the streets they sing, after all, people with disabilities
In the cold, hungry, grieving.

Careless persons, individuals,
Go to hell at least once a concert.
Singing in wheelchairs now disabled
Serve them at least your dessert!

Rahim Karim (Karimov)

Sujata
Paul

Sujata Pau

Sujata Paul is a poet and educator from Kolkata, India, who writes in Bengali, English and Hindi. Her poems and articles have been published in numerous anthologies like *Spilling Essences*, *I Am A Woman, Burning Desire, Daddy* (U. S Publications), *Queen, Family, Ripples Of Peace, The Spirit Of India, Gungunati Lehre, Are We Mere Spectators, Traumas On Widows, Pictorial Poetry, Social Media And Literature, Pros And Cons*, and *Complexion Based Discrimination*. Her first poetry book *Whisper Of My Soul* will be published soon.

Email: paul.megha65@gmail.com

Link: https://www.facebook.com/mithu.saha.7773631

Just Wanted This

Wanted this kind of pure rainfall
In which there would not be any acid or dirt
Only the purity that will wash all the garbage.

Just wanted an innocent heart
That will fill up the soul with love and affection
Where there would not be any artificiality.

Just wanted some kind of verses
Which won't attack or highlight one's own arrogance
Rather will show the way to proceed and spread the
delicious fragrance.

Just wanted this kind of selfless devotion
In which one could surrender themselves without any
hesitation.

Loop Poetry

Look at the girl
Girl is so innocent
Innocent by heart
Heart is full of love.

Love needs caring
Caring comes from the soul
Soul is immortal
Immortal is not human being.

Human beings are mysterious
Mysterious is their mind
Mind is faster than air
Air we need to live.

I Need Some Open Air

I need some open air
Nowadays I feel suffocated.

Light I need very much
For the darkness haunts me.

You know -
I wish to lean on you
To have some oxygen,
Hope to hug you tightly
So that no one could snatch me from you,
Wish to step together
To lead the journey of life,
Wish to jump over the sea of love
And float there up to eternity.
Again wish to have challenges
To test the intensity of your love.

Some open air and a ray of hope
Are needed very much
For I am scared of darkness and of suffocation.

Bharati Nayak

Bharati Nayak

Bharati Nayak,born in the year 1962 ,is a bilingual poet,critique and translator from Odisha,an Indian State lying on its eastern coast.She writes in English and Odia.Her poems have been published in many magazines,journals ,anthologies and e-books of national and international repute such as *Rock Pebbles,Orissa Review, Utkal Prasang, Creation and Criticism, Circular Whispers, Nova Literature-Poesis, PoetryAgaist Terror, 56 Female Voices of Poetry ,The Four Seasons Poetry Concerto, Tunes From the Subcontinent, Amaravati Poetic Prism, Bhubaneswar Review* and the like.

She has published three poetry books-
1-*Padma Paada*(A poetry book in Odia language)
2-*Words Are Such Perfect Traitors*
3-*A Day for Myself*

I Speak Not

I speak not
As I feel
Speaking is not essential.

Silence speaks for itself
Even eyes speak
Speak thousand words
My quivering lips.
Unsaid words travel million miles.

Sun speaks
Moon speaks
Speaks the thunderstorm
When hearts meet
Mouth says no words
Only the closeness knows
How louder is the heart
When it beats
Beating the loudness of sea roars.

Parrot

Though winged
I am caged
I flutter my wings
As if to fly
They get hurt by the iron railings.

The milked rice and good nuts
That I am served
Do not satisfy me
As dream of the open   sky
Where I   do belong.

You ask me
Oh Parrot ! How are you?
You see my bright   green feathers
And my beautiful red beak
I answer in my clatter
Which you can not understand
And think
I belong to the rich and
So I live in lavish.

On some careless day
My owner may
Keep the cage open
I may get a chance to fly
But my wings
That have forgotten
The art of flying
May fall a prey
To some vultures.

Bharati Nayak

My good owner and his neighbors
Will curse me and say
O.K. O.K.
Let that ungrateful bird
Meet a graceless end.

Sea and Seashore

You are the ocean, endless
I am but a tiny grain of sand
After being bathed countless times
By your great tides
Still wait for
Another countless baths.

Each tide
Like a dream
Attracts me to its heart
But, every time
I am thrown back
To the shore of day's reality.

My soul expands
To billions and billions of sand grains
Uniting with them
I become the sea-shore
Then I take your endlessness
In my embrace.

Bharati Nayak

Kapardeli
Eftichia

Kapardeli Eftichia has a Doctorate from ARTS and CULTURE WORLD ACADEMY She currently lives in Patras. She writes poetry, stories, short stories, hai-ku , essays. She studied journalism AKEM Has many awards in national competitions. Her work there is to many national and international anthologies.   She has a section at the University of Cyprus in Greek culture is a member of the world poets society. website is http://world-poets.blogspot. Com. She is a member of the IWA (international writers and artists Association); chaired by Teresinka Pereira; had from IWA Certify 2017 as the best translation and member of the POETAS DEL MUNDO .

kapardeli@gmail.com

https://www.facebook.com/PPdM.Mundial

https://twitter.com/Poetedumonde

http://eftichiakapa.blogspot.gr/2013_10_01_archive.html

http://isbn.nlg.gr/index.php?lvl=author_see&id=30410

https://www.facebook.com/kapardeli.eftichia

http://eftichiakapa.blogspot.gr/2013/08/blog-post_4143.html

http://worldpeaceacademy.blogspot.gr/2010/10/poets-for-world-peace.html

Myrrh of drunkenness

In the Immortal Earth
intoxicating joy and
fragrant charisma
of flowers pollen
***
Myrrh of drunkenness, secret
wavy hair
cravings hidden
with the kiss of the first
Sunlight morning
you
***
Excess affection
an intoxicating source
wavy dancing
in pleasure veil
Aura of simple joy,
Aura sun sculpture
Libation

ΜΥΡΟ ΤΗΣ ΜΕΘΗΣ

Στην Αθάνατη γη
μεθυστικής χαράς και
ευωδιάς χάρισμα
των ανθών η γύρη
***
Μύρο της μέθης μυστικό
μαλλιά κυματιστά
πόθοι κρυφοί
με το φιλί της πρώτης
αυγινής Ηλιαχτίδας εσύ
***
Περίσσεια στοργή
μεθυστική πηγή
κυματιστός χορός
σε πέπλο ηδονής
Αύρα της απλής
χαράς ,αύρα
ηλιόγλυπτης σπονδής

ΗΜΕΡΕΣ ΕΥΛΟΓΙΑΣ

Ημέρες ευλογίας
στα ασημένια φύλλα της
λεύκας που πλημμύρισαν τις
ακίνητες στέγες και τα παράθυρα
των σπιτιών με μυστικές ευχές

Ο δρόμος της ζωής μου
σε ένα μικρό σύμπαν
από φώς
στα δίκαια της ψυχής

Days of blessing . . . ME

Days of blessing
on silver leaves
of the poplar that flooded
the
immovable roofs and windows
of homes with secret wishes

The way of my life
in a small universe
from light
in the righteousness of the soul

ΛΕΥΚΗ ΣΙΩΠΗ

Δύο κόσμοι
που τυχαία συναντώνται
στην άγνοια των καιρών
χτίζουν και γκρεμίζουν
με την λευκή   σιωπή των χρόνων

Τριμμένες λέξεις ,μισοτελειωμένες φράσεις
σε μια ξεχασμένη γλώσσα
Όνειρα
Αναδύονται, χαράσσονται
στις γνώριμες ρυτίδες
στα ίδια χρόνια
που τα μάτια γέρασαν
στις μνήμες

White Silence

Two worlds
who accidentally   meet
in the ignorance of the times
build and shatter
with the white of the times silence

Grated words, half-finished phrases
in a forgotten tongue
Dreams
they emerge, they are engraved
to the intimate wrinkles
in the same years
which the eyes had grown old
on the edges memories

Heshtje E Bardhë

Dy botë
Që takohen rastësisht
Ndërtojnë dhe shëmbin
Me heshtjen e bardhë të viteve.
Fjalë të thërmuara, fraza gjysmë të mbaruara
Në një gjuhë të harruar.
Ëndrra shkridhen, vizohen
Në rrudhat e njohura
Në të njëjzët vite
Kur sytë u plakën në kujtesë.

ΝΕΕΣ ΑΧΤΙΝΕΣ

Ένα φιλί και ένα όνειρο
τραυματισμένα
στις γωνιές της νύχτας ξεχασμένα
χρυσαλίδες χρωματισμένες ,μεταξένιες
μπερδεμένες φωσφορίζουν φυλακισμένες

Γυμνοί οι δρόμοι
τα μάτια δεν μπορούν να αποδράσουν
ψάχνω το φως
πλάσματα Αγγελικά με μαλλιά πλεγμένα
σε άκρα ηδονή θείων σωμάτων
Λουσμένα

Στο περίγραμμα του κύκλου
Νέες Αχτίνες
στου κύκνου τα λευκά
φτερά γεννιούνται
στο ξεκίνημα της μέρας

New Rays

A kiss and a dream
injured
in the corners of the night forgotten
Colorful golden chrysalides
silky
confused phosphoresis, prisoners
The streets naked
the eyes can not escape
I'm looking for light
Angelic creatures with braided hair
at the end of pleasure of the divine bodies
bathed
On the outline of the circle
New rays
in the swan the white ones
wings are born
at the beginning of the day

Remembering

our fallen soldiers of verse

Janet Perkins Caldwell
February 14, 1959 ~ September 20, 2016

Alan W. Jankowski
16 March 1961 ~ 10 March 2017

Coming
April 2020

The
World Healing, World Peace
International Poetry Symposium

Stay Tuned

for more information
intouch@innerchildpress.com
'building bridges of cultural understanding'
www.innerchildpress.com

Inner Child Press

News

Poetry Posse Members

We are so excited to share and announce a few of the current books, as well as the new and upcoming books of some of our Poetry Posse authors.

On the following pages we present to you ...

Jackie Davis Allen

Gail Weston Shazor

hülya n. yılmaz

Nizar Sartawi

Faleeha Hassan

Fahredin Shehu

Caroline 'Ceri' Nazareno

Eliza Segiet

William S. Peters, Sr.

No Illusions

Through the Looking Glass

Jackie Davis Allen

Now Available at
www.innerchildpress.com

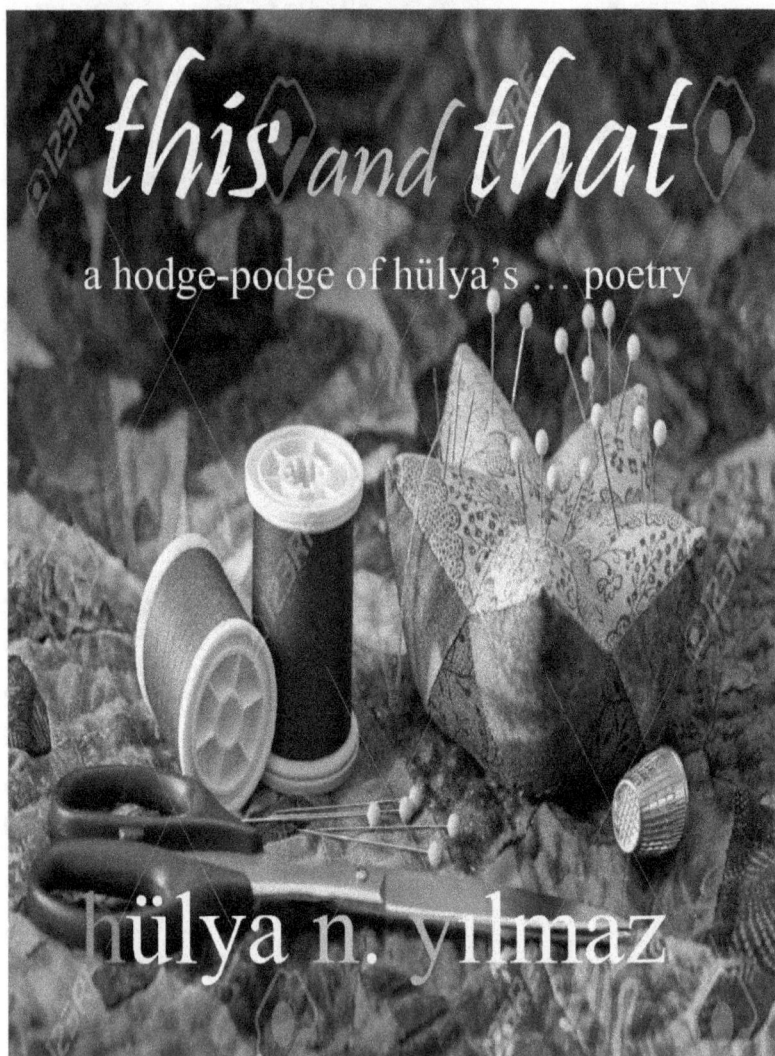

this and that

a hodge-podge of hülya's ... poetry

hülya n. yılmaz

Now Available at
www.innerchildpress.com

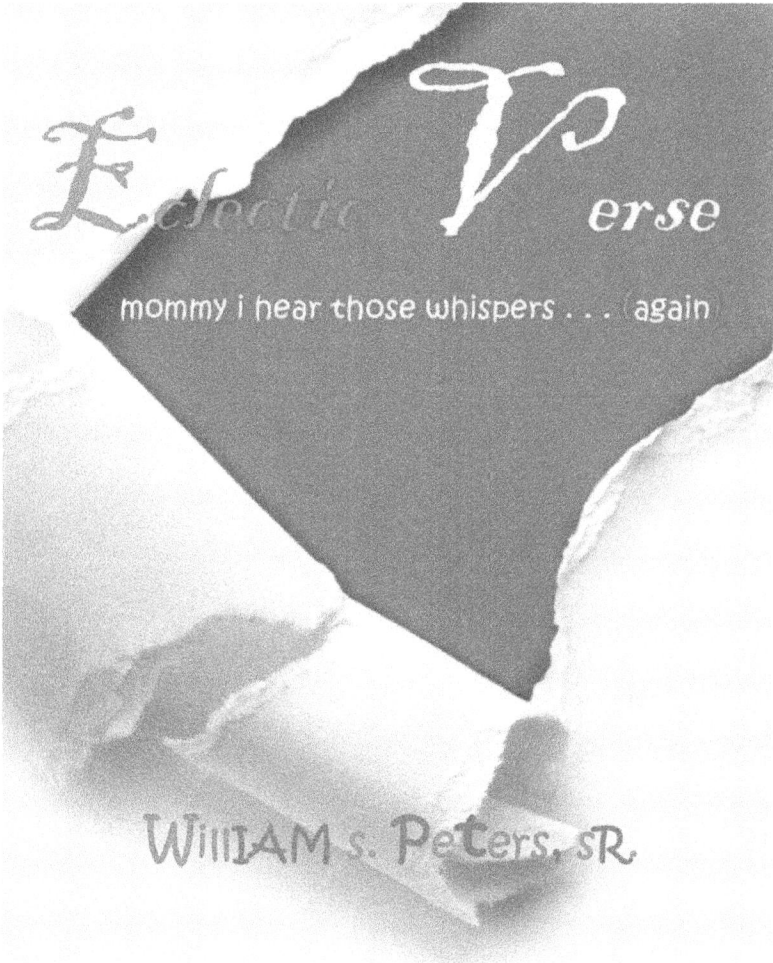

Inner Child Press News

Now Available at
www.innerchildpress.com

HERENOW

FAHREDIN SHEHU

Now Available at
www.innerchildpress.com

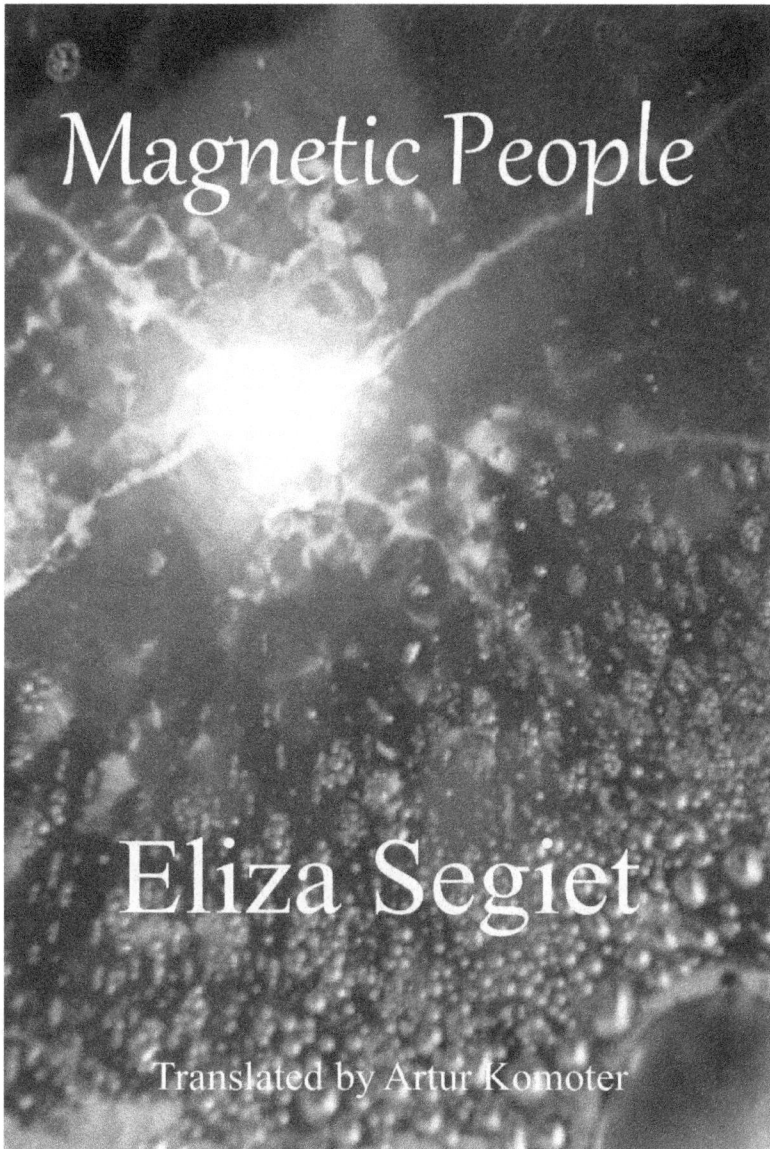

Magnetic People

Eliza Segiet

Translated by Artur Komoter

Now Available at
www.innerchildpress.com

Dark Side
of the
Moon

Jackie Davis Allen

Now Available at
www.innerchildpress.com

Now Available at
www.innerchildpress.com

Now Available at
www.innerchildpress.com

My Shadow

Nizar Sartawi

Mass Graves

Faleeha Hassan

Now Available at
www.innerchildpress.com

Breakfast

for

Butterflies

Faleeha Hassan

Now Available at
www.innerchildpress.com

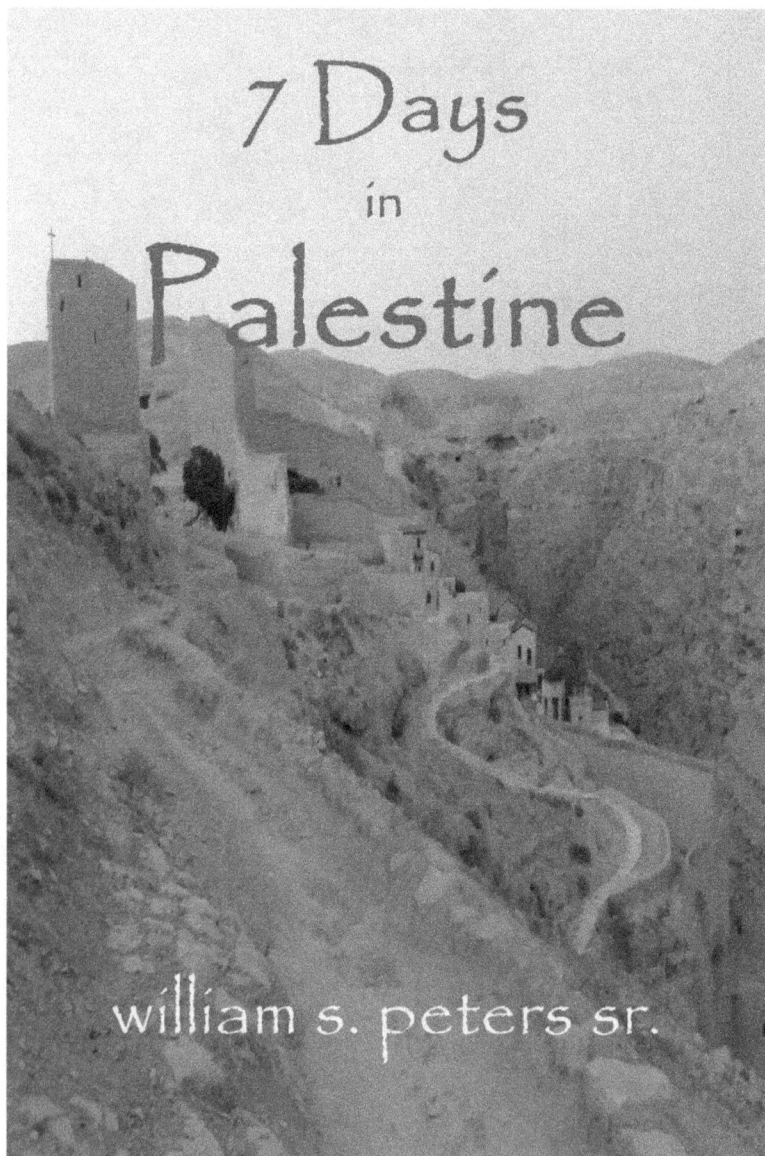

7 Days
in
Palestine

william s. peters sr.

Now Available at
www.innerchildpress.com

inner child press
presents

Tunisia My Love

william s. peters, sr.

Coming in the Summer of 2019

The Journey

Footprints and Shadows

Kosovo

Tunisia

Macedonia

Morocco

Jordan

Palestine

Israel

Italy

Turkey

a collection of poetry inspired during my travels

william s. peters, sr.

Now Available at
www.innerchildpress.com

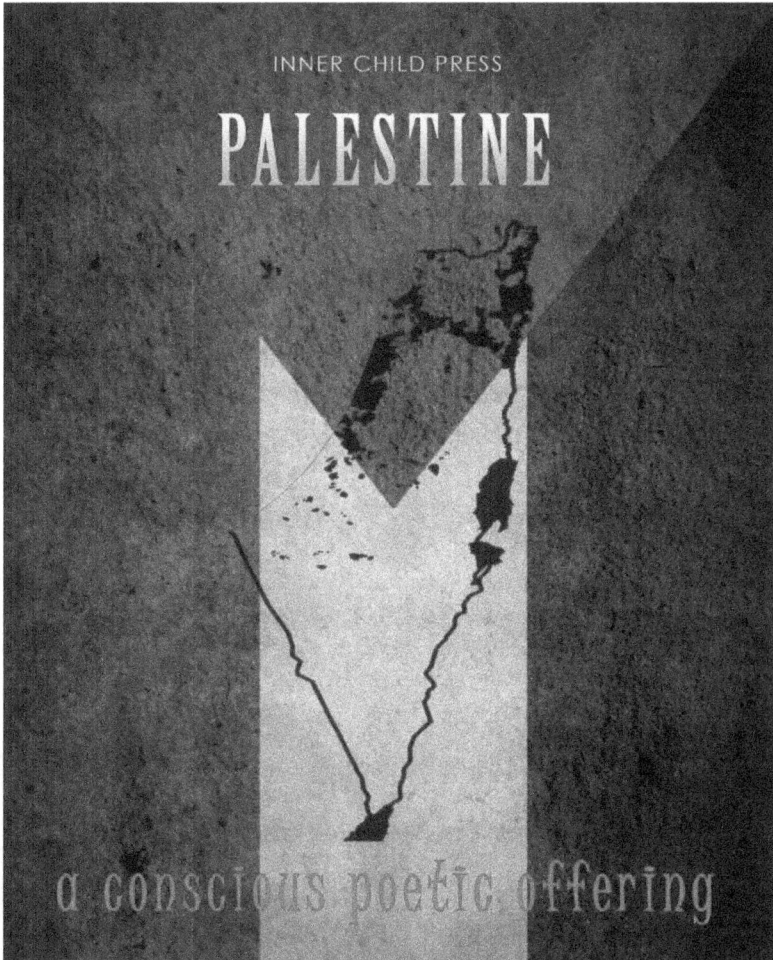

Now Available at
www.innerchildpress.com

Now Available at

www.innerchildpress.com

Now Available at
www.innerchildpress.com

Inward Reflections

This could work...

Yes...

I got it...

Ohh...

Think on These Things
Book II

william s. peters, sr.

Now Available at
www.innerchildpress.com

Poetry
from the
Balkans

The Balkan Poets

Other

Anthological

works from

Inner Child Press International

www.innerchildpress.com

Inner Child Press International
presents

A Love Anthology
2019

The Love Poets

Now Available

www.worldhealingworldpeacepoetry.com

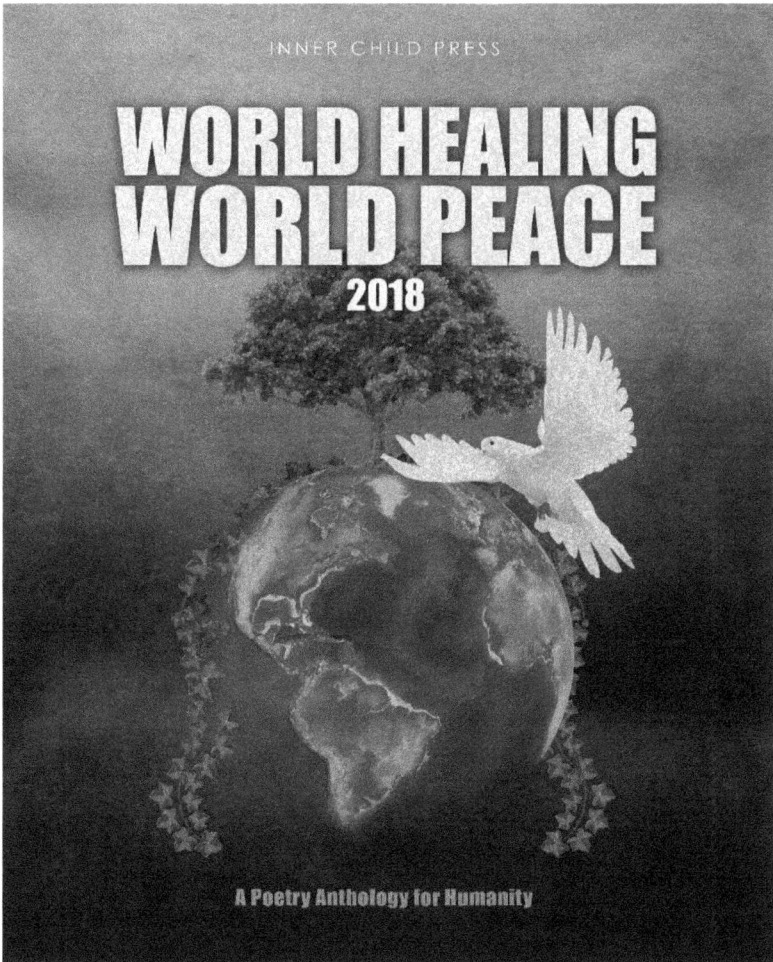

INNER CHILD PRESS

WORLD HEALING WORLD PEACE
2018

A Poetry Anthology for Humanity

Now Available

www.worldhealingworldpeacepoetry.com

Now Available

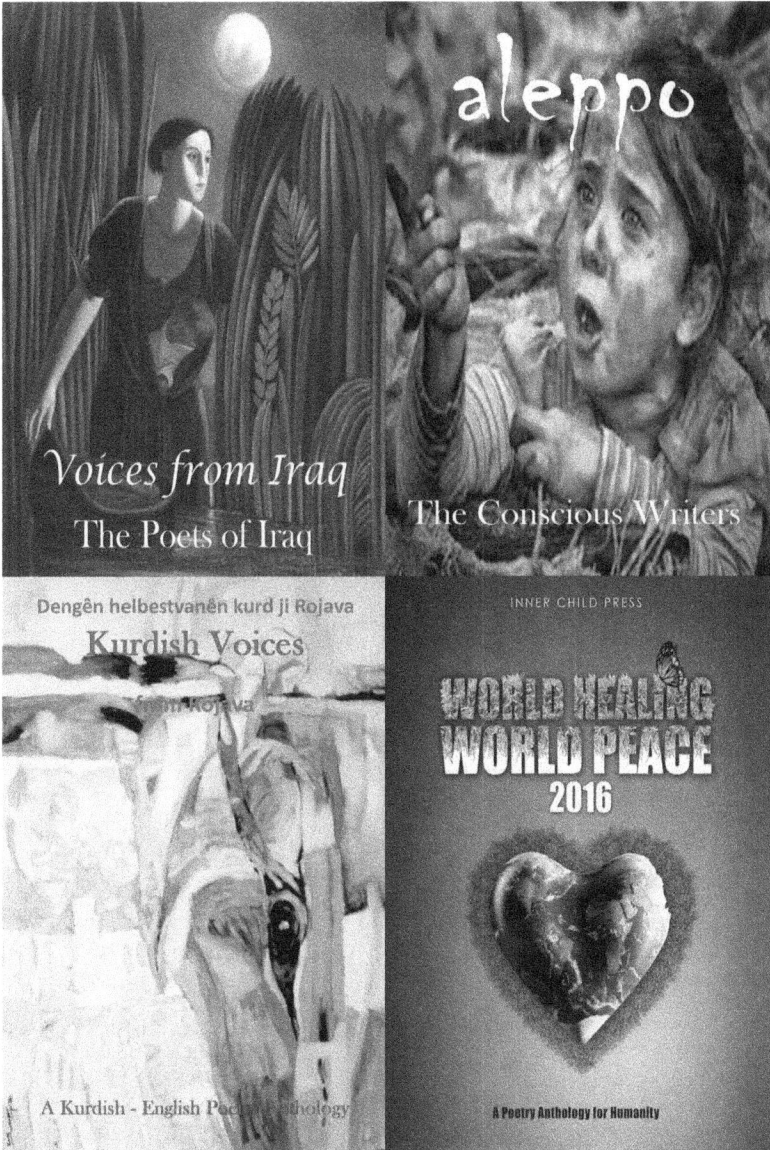

Now Available

www.innerchildpress.com/anthologies

Now Available

176

a collection of the Voices of Many inspired by . . .

Monte Smith

i want my

PoEtRy

to . . .

volume II

a collection of the Voices of Many inspired by . . .

Monte Smith

i want my

Poetry

to . . . volume 3

a collection of the Voices of Many inspired by . . .

Monte Smith

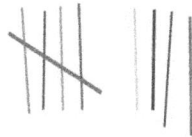

11 Words

(9 lines . . .)

for those who are challenged

an anthology of Poetry inspired by . . .

Poetry Dancer

Now Available

www.innerchildpress.com/anthologies

The Year of the Poet
January 2014

The Poetry Posse

Jamie Bond
Gail Weston Shazor
Albert 'Infinite' Carrasco
Siddartha Beth Pierce
Janet P. Caldwell
June 'Bugg' Barefield
Debbie M. Allen
Tony Henninger
Joe DaVerbal Minddancer
Robert Gibbons
Neeta Wali
Shareef Abdur-Rasheed
William S. Peters, Sr.

Carnation

Our January Feature
Terri L. Johnson

the Year of the Poet
February 2014

violets

The Poetry Posse
Jamie Bond
Gail Weston Shazor
Albert 'Infinite' Carrasco
Siddartha Beth Pierce
Janet P. Caldwell
June 'Bugg' Barefield
Debbie M. Allen
Tony Henninger
Joe DaVerbal Minddancer
Robert Gibbons
Neeta Wali
Shareef Abdur-Rasheed
William S. Peters, Sr.

Our February Features
Teresa E. Gallion & Robert Gibson

the Year of the Poet
March 2014

The Poetry Posse
Jamie Bond
Gail Weston Shazor
Albert 'Infinite' Carrasco
Siddartha Beth Pierce
Janet P. Caldwell
June 'Bugg' Barefield
Debbie M Allen
Tony Henninger
Joe DaVerbal Minddancer
Robert Gibbons
Neeta Wali
Shareef Abdur-Rasheed
Kimberly Burnham
William S. Peters, Sr.

daffodil

Our March Featured Poets
Alicia C. Cooper & hülya yılmaz

the Year of the Poet
April 2014

The Poetry Posse
Jamie Bond
Gail Weston Shazor
Albert 'Infinite' Carrasco
Siddartha Beth Pierce
Janet P. Caldwell
June 'Bugg' Barefield
Debbie M. Allen
Tony Henninger
Joe DaVerbal Minddancer
Robert Gibbons
Neeta Wali
Shareef Abdur-Rasheed
Kimberly Burnham
William S. Peters, Sr.

Our April Featured Poets
Fahredin Shehu
Martina Reisz Newberry
Justin Blackburn
Monte Smith

Sweet Pea

celebrating international poetry month

Now Available

www.innerchildpress.com/the-year-of-the-poet

Now Available

www.innerchildpress.com/the-year-of-the-poet

The Year of the Poet
September 2014

Aster **Morning-Glory**

Wild Chart of September Birthday Flower

September Feature Poets
Florence Maloine * Keith Alan Hamilton

The Poetry Posse
Jamie Bond * Gail Weston Shazor * Albert 'Infinite' Carrasco * Siddartha Beth Pierce
Janet P. Caldwell * June 'Bugg' Barefield * Debbie M. Allen * Tony Henninger
Joe DaVerbal Minddancer * Robert Gibbons * Neetu Wali * Shareef Abdur-Rasheed
Kimberly Burnham * William S. Peters, Sr.

THE YEAR OF THE POET
October 2014

Red Poppy

The Poetry Posse
Jamie Bond * Gail Weston Shazor * Albert 'Infinite' Carrasco * Siddartha Beth Pierce
Janet P. Caldwell * June 'Bugg' Barefield * Debbie M. Allen * Tony Henninger
Joe DaVerbal Minddancer * Robert Gibbons * Neetu Wali * Shareef Abdur-Rasheed
Kimberly Burnham * William S. Peters, Sr.

October Feature Poets
Ceri Naz * RaJendra Padhi * Elizabeth Castillo

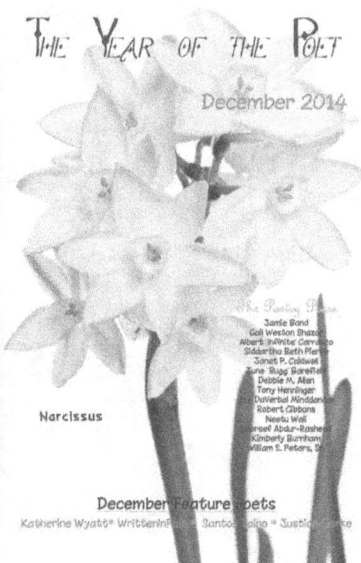

THE YEAR OF THE POET
November 2014

Chrysanthemum

The Poetry Posse
Jamie Bond * Gail Weston Shazor * Albert 'Infinite' Carrasco * Siddartha Beth Pierce
Janet P. Caldwell * June 'Bugg' Barefield * Debbie M. Allen * Tony Henninger
Joe DaVerbal Minddancer * Robert Gibbons * Neetu Wali * Shareef Abdur-Rasheed
Kimberly Burnham * William S. Peters, Sr.

November Feature Poets
Jocelyn Mosman * Jackie Allen * James Moore * Neville Hiatt

THE YEAR OF THE POET
December 2014

Narcissus

The Poetry Posse
Jamie Bond
Gail Weston Shazor
Albert 'Infinite' Carrasco
Siddartha Beth Pierce
Janet P. Caldwell
June 'Bugg' Barefield
Debbie M. Allen
Tony Henninger
DaVerbal Minddancer
Robert Gibbons
Neetu Wali
Shareef Abdur-Rasheed
Kimberly Burnham
William S. Peters, Sr.

December Feature Poets
Katherine Wyatt* WrittenInkPoet* Santoci Laine * Justin Blake

Now Available

www.innerchildpress.com/the-year-of-the-poet

THE YEAR OF THE POET II
January 2015

Garnet

The Poetry Posse
Jamie Bond
Gail Weston Shazor
Albert 'Infinite' Carrasco
Siddartha Beth Pierce
Janet P. Caldwell
Tony Henninger
Joe DaVerbal Minddancer
Robert Gibbons
Neetu Wali
Shareef Abdur – Rasheed
Kimberly Burnham
Ann White
Keith Alan Hamilton
Katherine Wyatt
Fahredin Shehu
Hülya N. Yılmaz
Teresa E. Gallion
Jackie Allen
William S. Peters, Sr.

January Feature Poets
Bismay Mohanti * Jen Walls * Eric Judah

THE YEAR OF THE POET II
February 2015

Amethyst

THE POETRY POSSE
Jamie Bond
Gail Weston Shazor
Albert 'Infinite' Carrasco
Siddartha Beth Pierce
Janet P. Caldwell
Tony Henninger
Joe DaVerbal Minddancer
Robert Gibbons
Neetu Wali
Shareef Abdur – Rasheed
Kimberly Burnham
Ann White
Keith Alan Hamilton
Katherine Wyatt
Fahredin Shehu
Hülya N. Yılmaz
Teresa E. Gallion
Jackie Allen
William S. Peters, Sr.

FEBRUARY FEATURE POETS
Iram Fatima * Bob McNeil * Kerstin Centervall

The Year of the Poet II
March 2015

Our Featured Poets
Heung Sook * Anthony Arnold * Alicia Poland

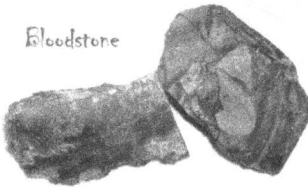

Bloodstone

The Poetry Posse 2015
Jamie Bond * Gail Weston Shazor * Albert 'Infinite' Carrasco
Siddartha Beth Pierce * Janet P. Caldwell * Tony Henninger
Joe DaVerbal Minddancer * Neetu Wali * Shareef Abdur – Rasheed
Kimberly Burnham * Ann White * Keith Alan Hamilton
Katherine Wyatt * Fahredin Shehu * Hülya N. Yılmaz
Teresa E. Gallion * Jackie Allen * William S. Peters, Sr

The Year of the Poet II
April 2015
Celebrating International Poetry Month

Our Featured Poets
Raja Williams * Dennis Ferado * Laure Charazac

Diamonds

The Poetry Posse 2015
Jamie Bond * Gail Weston Shazor * Albert 'Infinite' Carrasco
Siddartha Beth Pierce * Janet P. Caldwell * Tony Henninger
Joe DaVerbal Minddancer * Neetu Wali * Shareef Abdur – Rasheed
Kimberly Burnham * Ann White * Keith Alan Hamilton
Katherine Wyatt * Fahredin Shehu * Hülya N. Yılmaz
Teresa E. Gallion * Jackie Allen * William S. Peters, Sr

Now Available

www.innerchildpress.com/the-year-of-the-poet

The Year of the Poet II
May 2015

May's Featured Poets
Geri Algeri
Akin Mosi Chinnery
Anna Jakubcza

Emeralds

The Poetry Posse 2015
Jamie Bond * Gail Weston Shazor * Albert 'Infinite' Carrasco
Siddartha Beth Pierce * Janet P. Caldwell * Tony Henninger
Joe DaVerbal Minddancer * Neetu Wali * Shareef Abdur – Rasheed
Kimberly Burnham * Ann White * Keith Alan Hamilton
Katherine Wyatt * Fahredin Shehu * Hülya N. Yılmaz
Teresa E. Gallion * Jackie Allen * William S. Peters, Sr.

The Year of the Poet II
June 2015

June's Featured Poets
Anahit Arustamyan * Yvette D. Murrell * Regina A. Walker

Pearl

The Poetry Posse 2015
Jamie Bond * Gail Weston Shazor * Albert 'Infinite' Carrasco
Siddartha Beth Pierce * Janet P. Caldwell * Tony Henninger
Joe DaVerbal Minddancer * Neetu Wali * Shareef Abdur – Rasheed
Kimberly Burnham * Ann White * Keith Alan Hamilton
Katherine Wyatt * Fahredin Shehu * Hülya N. Yılmaz
Teresa E. Gallion * Jackie Allen * William S. Peters, Sr.

The Year of the Poet II
July 2015

The Featured Poets for July 2015
Abhik Shome * Christina Neal * Robert Neal

Rubies

The Poetry Posse 2015
Jamie Bond * Gail Weston Shazor * Albert 'Infinite' Carrasco
Siddartha Beth Pierce * Janet P. Caldwell * Tony Henninger
Joe DaVerbal Minddancer * Neetu Wali * Shareef Abdur – Rasheed
Kimberly Burnham * Ann White * Keith Alan Hamilton
Katherine Wyatt * Fahredin Shehu * Hülya N. Yılmaz
Teresa E. Gallion * Jackie Allen * William S. Peters, Sr.

The Year of the Poet II
August 2015

Peridot

Featured Poets
Gayle Howell
Ann Chalasz
Christopher Schultz

The Poetry Posse 2015
Jamie Bond * Gail Weston Shazor * Albert 'Infinite' Carrasco
Siddartha Beth Pierce * Janet P. Caldwell * Tony Henninger
Joe DaVerbal Minddancer * Neetu Wali * Shareef Abdur – Rasheed
Kimberly Burnham * Ann White * Keith Alan Hamilton
Katherine Wyatt * Fahredin Shehu * Hülya N. Yılmaz
Teresa E. Gallion * Jackie Allen * William S. Peters, Sr.

Now Available

www.innerchildpress.com/the-year-of-the-poet

The Year of the Poet II
September 2015

Featured Poets

Alfreda Ghee   Lonneice Weeks Badley   Demetrios Trifiatis

Sapphires

The Poetry Posse 2015

Jamie Bond * Gail Weston Shazor * Albert 'Infinite' Carrasco
Siddartha Beth Pierce * Janet P. Caldwell * Tony Henninger
Joe DaVerbal Minddancer * Neetu Wali * Shareef Abdur – Rasheed
Kimberly Burnham * Ann White * Keith Alan Hamilton
Katherine Wyatt * Fahredin Shehu * Hülya N. Yılmaz
Teresa E. Gallion * Jackie Allen * William S. Peters, Sr

The Year of the Poet II
October 2015

Featured Poets

Monte Smith * Laura J. Wolfe * William Washington

Opal

The Poetry Posse 2015

Jamie Bond * Gail Weston Shazor * Albert 'Infinite' Carrasco
Siddartha Beth Pierce * Janet P. Caldwell * Tony Henninger
Joe DaVerbal Minddancer * Neetu Wali * Shareef Abdur – Rasheed
Kimberly Burnham * Ann White * Keith Alan Hamilton
Katherine Wyatt * Fahredin Shehu * Hülya N. Yılmaz
Teresa E. Gallion * Jackie Allen * William S. Peters, Sr.

The Year of the Poet II
November 2015

Featured Poets

Alan W. Jankowski
Hismay Mohanty
James Moore

Topaz

The Poetry Posse 2015

Jamie Bond * Gail Weston Shazor * Albert 'Infinite' Carrasco
Siddartha Beth Pierce * Janet P. Caldwell * Tony Henninger
Joe DaVerbal Minddancer * Neetu Wali * Shareef Abdur – Rasheed
Kimberly Burnham * Ann White * Keith Alan Hamilton
Katherine Wyatt * Fahredin Shehu * Hülya N. Yılmaz
Teresa E. Gallion * Jackie Allen * William S. Peters, Sr.

The Year of the Poet II
December 2015

Featured Poets

Kerione Bryan * Michelle Joan Barulich * Neville Hiatt

Turquoise

The Poetry Posse 2015

Jamie Bond * Gail Weston Shazor * Albert 'Infinite' Carrasco
Siddartha Beth Pierce * Janet P. Caldwell * Tony Henninger
Joe DaVerbal Minddancer * Neetu Wali * Shareef Abdur – Rasheed
Kimberly Burnham * Ann White * Keith Alan Hamilton
Katherine Wyatt * Fahredin Shehu * Hülya N. Yılmaz
Teresa E. Gallion * Jackie Allen * William S. Peters, Sr.

Now Available

www.innerchildpress.com/the-year-of-the-poet

Now Available

www.innerchildpress.com/the-year-of-the-poet

The Year of the Poet — May 2016

Bob Strum
Barbara Allan
D.L. Davis

Oriole

The Poetry Posse 2016

The Year of the Poet III — June 2016

Featured Poets

Qibrije Demiri- Frangu
Naime Beqiraj
Faleeha Hassan
Bedri Zyberaj

Black Necked Stilt

The Poetry Posse 2016

The Year of the Poet — July 2016

Featured Poets

Tram Fatima 'Ashi'
Langley Shazor
Jody Doty
Emilia T. Davis

Indigo Bunting

The Poetry Posse 2016

The Year of the Poet III — August 2016

Featured Poets

Anita Dash
Irena Jovanovic
Malgorzata Gouluda

Painted Bunting

The Poetry Posse 2016

Now Available

www.innerchildpress.com/the-year-of-the-poet

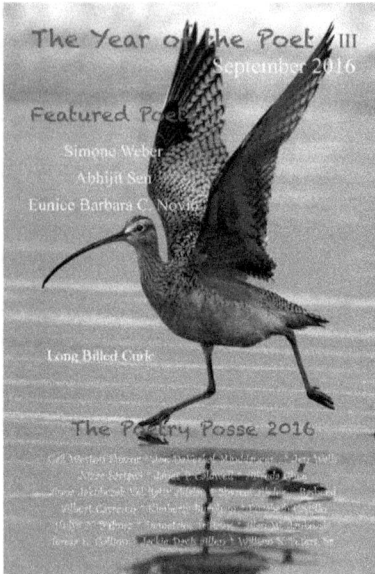

The Year of the Poet III
September 2016

Featured Poets
Simone Weber
Abhijit Sen
Eunice Barbara C. Novio

Long Billed Curle

The Poetry Posse 2016

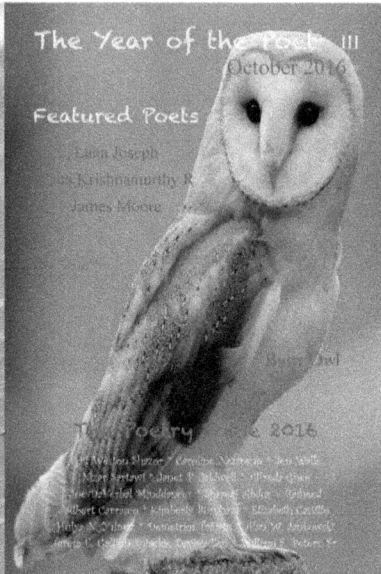

The Year of the Poet III
October 2016

Featured Poets
Liana Joseph
Krishnamurthy K
James Moore

Barn Owl

The Poetry Posse 2016

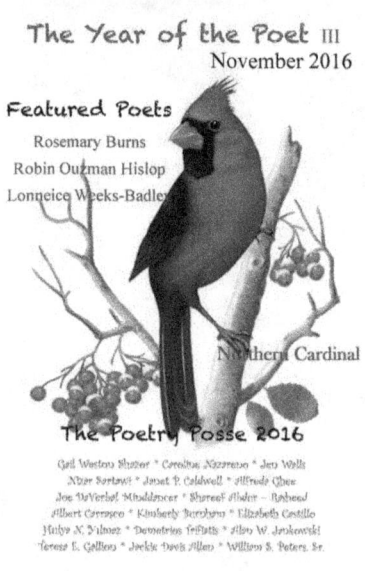

The Year of the Poet III
November 2016

Featured Poets
Rosemary Burns
Robin Ouzman Hislop
Lonneice Weeks-Badler

Northern Cardinal

The Poetry Posse 2016

Gail Weston Shazor * Caroline Nazareno * Jen Walls
Nizar Sartawi * Janet P. Caldwell * Alfreda Ghee
Joe DaVerbal Minddancer * Shareef Abdur – Rasheed
Albert Carrasco * Kimberly Burnham * Elizabeth Castillo
Hülya N. Yılmaz * Demetrios Trifiatis * Allen W. Jankowski
Teresa E. Gallion * Jackie Davis Allen * William S. Peters, Sr.

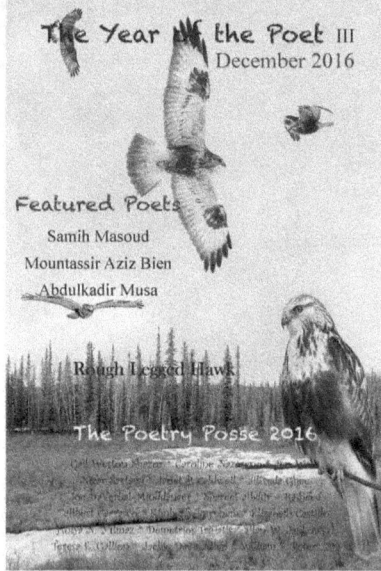

The Year of the Poet III
December 2016

Featured Poets
Samih Masoud
Mountassir Aziz Bien
Abdulkadir Musa

Rough Legged Hawk

The Poetry Posse 2016

Now Available

www.innerchildpress.com/the-year-of-the-poet

The Year of the Poet IV
January 2017

Featured Poets
Jon Winell
Natalie Shields
Jamil Fatima 'Aziz

Quaking Aspen

The Poetry Posse 2017

Gail Weston Shazor * Caroline Nazareno * Birunji Mohanty
Nizar Sartawi * Jossa Jakabcsin Vel Betty Jidalan * Jen Walls
Joe DaVerbal Minddancer * Shareef Abdur - Rasheed
Albert Carrasco * Kimberly Burnham * Elizabeth Castillo
Hulya N. Yilmaz * Teleaha Hassan * Allan W. Jaskowski
Teresa E. Gallion * Jackie Davis Allen * William S. Peters, Sr

The Year of the Poet IV
February 2017

Featured Poets
Lin Ross
Souleima Falhi
Anwer Ghani

Witch Hazel

The Poetry Posse 2017

Gail Weston Shazor * Caroline Nazareno * Birunji Mohanty
Nizar Sartawi * Jossa Jakabcsin Vel Betty Jidalan * Jen Walls
Joe DaVerbal Minddancer * Shareef Abdur - Rasheed
Albert Carrasco * Kimberly Burnham * Elizabeth Castillo
Hulya N. Yilmaz * Teleaha Hassan * allan W. Jaskowski
Teresa E. Gallion * Jackie Davis Allen * William S. Peters, Sr

The Year of the Poet IV
March 2017

Featured Poets
Tremell Stevens
Francisca Ricinski
Jamil Abu Shaih

The Eastern Redbud

The Poetry Posse 2017

Gail Weston Shazor * Caroline Nazareno * Birunji Mohanty
Teresa E. Gallion * Jossa Jakabcsin Vel Betty Jidalan
Joe DaVerbal Minddancer * Shareef Abdur - Rasheed
Albert Carrasco * Kimberly Burnham * Elizabeth Castillo
Hulya N. Yilmaz * Teleaha Hassan * Jackie Davis Allen
Jen Walls * Nizar Sartawi * William S. Peters, Sr

The Year of the Poet IV
April 2017

Featured Poets
Dr. Rachida Barman
Neptune Barman
Masoud Khabif

The Blossoming Cherry

The Poetry Posse 2017

Gail Weston Shazor * Caroline Nazareno * Birunji Mohanty
Teresa E. Gallion * Jossa Jakabcsin Vel Betty Jidalan
Joe DaVerbal Minddancer * Shareef Abdur - Rasheed
Albert Carrasco * Kimberly Burnham * Elizabeth Castillo
Hulya N. Yilmaz * Teleaha Hassan * Jackie Davis Allen
Jen Walls * Nizar Sartawi * William S. Peters, Sr

Now Available

www.innerchildpress.com/the-year-of-the-poet

The Year of the Poet IV
May 2017

The Flowering Dogwood Tree

Featured Poets
Kallisa Powell
Alicja Maria Kuberska
Fethi Sassi

The Poetry Posse 2017

Gail Weston Shazor * Caroline Nazareno * Jhimey Mohanty
Teresa E. Gallion * Anna Jakubczak Vel Ratty Adalan
Joe DeVerbel Misddancer * Shareef Abdur – Rasheed
Albert Carrasco * Kimberly Burnham * Elizabeth Castillo
Hülya N. Yılmaz * Falesha Hassan * Jackie Davis Allen
Jen Wells * Nizar Sartawi * * William S. Peters, Sr.

The Year of the Poet IV
June 2017

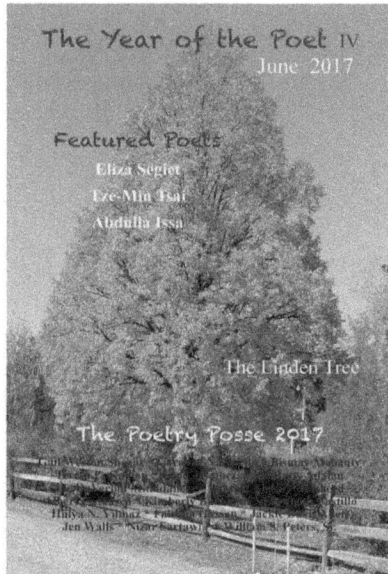

Featured Poets
Eliza Segiet
Eze-Min Tsai
Abdulla Issa

The Linden Tree

The Poetry Posse 2017

Hülya N. Yılmaz *
Jen Wells * Nizar Sartawi * William S. Peters,

The Year of the Poet IV
July 2017

Featured Poets
Anca Mihaela Bruma
Ibaa Ismail
Zvonko Taneski

The Oak Moon

The Poetry Posse 2017

The Year of the Poet IV
August 2017

Featured Poets
Jonathan Aquino
Kitty Hsu
Langley Shazor

The Hazelnut Tree

The Poetry Posse 2017

Gail Weston Shazor * Caroline Nazareno *
Teresa E. Gallion * Anna Jakubczak Vel Ratty Adalan
Joe DeVerbel Misddancer * Shareef Abdur – Rasheed
Albert Carrasco * Kimberly Burnham * Elizabeth Castillo
Hülya N. Yılmaz * Falesha Hassan * Jackie Davis Allen
Jen Wells * Nizar Sartawi * * William S. Peters, Sr.

Now Available

www.innerchildpress.com/the-year-of-the-poet

The Year of the Poet IV
September 2017

Featured Poets

Martina Reisz Newberry

Ameer Nassir

Christine Fulco Neal

Robert Neal

The Elm Tree

The Poetry Posse 2017

Gail Weston Shazor * Caroline Nazareno * Bismay Mohanty
Teresa E. Gallion * Anna Jakubczak Vel Ratty Adalan
Joe DaVerbal Minddancer * Shareef Abdur – Rasheed
Albert Carrasco * Kimberly Burnham * Elizabeth Castillo
Hülya N. Yılmaz * Faleeha Hassan * Jackie Davis Allen
Jen Walls * Nizar Sartawi * * William S. Peters, Sr.

The Year of the Poet IV
October 2017

Featured Poets

Ahmed Abu Saleem

Nedal Al-Qaeim

Sadeddin Shahin

The Black Walnut Tree

The Poetry Posse 2017

Gail Weston Shazor * Caroline Nazareno * Bismay Mohanty
Teresa E. Gallion * Anna Jakubczak Vel Ratty Adalan
Joe DaVerbal Minddancer * Shareef Abdur – Rasheed
Albert Carrasco * Kimberly Burnham * Elizabeth Castillo
Hülya N. Yılmaz * Faleeha Hassan * Jackie Davis Allen
Jen Walls * Nizar Sartawi * * William S. Peters, Sr.

The Year of the Poet IV
November 2017

Featured Poets

Kay Peters

Alfreda D. Ghee

Gabriella Garofalo

Rosemary Cappello

The Tree of Life

The Poetry Posse 2017

Gail Weston Shazor * Caroline Nazareno * Bismay Mohanty
Teresa E. Gallion * Anna Jakubczak Vel Ratty Adalan
Joe DaVerbal Minddancer * Shareef Abdur – Rasheed
Albert Carrasco * Kimberly Burnham * Elizabeth Castillo
Hülya N. Yılmaz * Faleeha Hassan * Jackie Davis Allen
Jen Walls * Nizar Sartawi * William S. Peters, Sr.

The Year of the Poet IV
December 2017

Featured Poets

Justice Clarke

Mariel M. Pabroa

Kiley Brown

The Fig Tree

The Poetry Posse 2017

Gail Weston Shazor * Caroline Nazareno * Bismay Mohanty
Teresa E. Gallion * Anna Jakubczak Vel Ratty Adalan
Joe DaVerbal Minddancer * Shareef Abdur – Rasheed
Albert Carrasco * Kimberly Burnham * Elizabeth Castillo
Hülya N. Yılmaz * Faleeha Hassan * Jackie Davis Allen
Jen Walls * Nizar Sartawi * William S. Peters, Sr.

Now Available

www.innerchildpress.com/the-year-of-the-poet

The Year of the Poet V
January 2018
Featured Poets
Iyad Shamasnah
Yasmeen Hamzeh
Ali Abdolrezaei

Aksum

The Poetry Posse 2018
Gail Weston Shazor * Caroline Nazareno * Tezmin Ition Tsai
Hülya N. Yılmaz * Faleeha Hassan * Jackie Davis Allen
Teresa E. Gallion * Anna Jakubczak Vel Ratty Adalan
Alicja Maria Kuberska * Shareef Abdur – Rasheed
Kimberly Burnham * Elizabeth Castillo
Nizar Sartawi * William S. Peters, Sr.

The Year of the Poet V
February 2018

Sabean

Featured Poets
Muhammad Azram
Anna Szawracka
Abhilipsa Kuanar
Aanika Aery

The Poetry Posse 2018
Gail Weston Shazor * Caroline Nazareno * Tezmin Ition Tsai
Hülya N. Yılmaz * Faleeha Hassan * Jackie Davis Allen
Teresa E. Gallion * Anna Jakubczak Vel Ratty Adalan
Alicja Maria Kuberska * Shareef Abdur – Rasheed
Kimberly Burnham * Elizabeth Castillo
Nizar Sartawi * William S. Peters, Sr.

The Year of the Poet V
March 2018

Featured Poets
Iram Fatima 'Ashi'
Cassandra Swan
Jaleel Khazaal
Shazia Zaman

Mexico   Cuba

Caribbean
&
Middle America

The Poetry Posse 2018
Gail Weston Shazor * Nizar Sartawi * Hülya N. Yılmaz
Jackie Davis Allen * Caroline 'Ceri' Nazareno
Alicja Maria Kuberska * Teresa E. Gallion
Faleeha Hassan * Shareef Abdur – Rasheed
Kimberly Burnham * Elizabeth Castillo
Tezmin Ition Tsai * William S. Peters, Sr.

The Year of the Poet V
April 2018

Featured Poets

The Nez Perce

The Poetry Posse 2018

Now Available

www.innerchildpress.com/the-year-of-the-poet

The Year of the Poet V
May 2018

Featured Poets

Zak.y Canyon de Leon Jr
Sylwia K. Malinowska
Liudna Ahmeti
Oleha Poshin

The Sumerians

The Poetry Posse 2018

Gail Weston Shazor * Nizar Sartawi * Hülya N. Yilmaz
Jackie Davis Allen * Caroline 'Ceri' Nazareno
Alicja Maria Kubenska * Teresa E. Gallion
Kimberly Burnham * Shareef Abdur – Rasheed
Faleeha Hassan * Elizabeth Castillo * Swapna Behera
Tezmin Ition Tsai * William S. Peters, Sr.

The Year of the Poet V
June 2018

Featured Poets

Bilall Maliqi * Daim Mihari * Gojko Božović * Sofija Živković

The Paleo Indians

The Poetry Posse 2018

Gail Weston Shazor * Nizar Sartawi * Hülya N. Yilmaz
Jackie Davis Allen * Caroline 'Ceri' Nazareno
Alicja Maria Kubenska * Teresa E. Gallion
Kimberly Burnham * Shareef Abdur – Rasheed
Faleeha Hassan * Elizabeth Castillo * Swapna Behera
Tezmin Ition Tsai * William S. Peters, Sr.

The Year of the Poet V
July 2018

Featured Poets
Fatimah Irmizat-Paddy
Mohammad Ikbal Hardi
Eliza Seglet
Tom Higgins

Oceania

The Poetry Posse 2018

Gail Weston Shazor * Nizar Sartawi * Hülya N. Yilmaz
Jackie Davis Allen * Caroline 'Ceri' Nazareno
Alicja Maria Kubenska * Teresa E. Gallion
Kimberly Burnham * Shareef Abdur – Rasheed
Faleeha Hassan * Elizabeth Castillo * Swapna Behera
Tezmin Ition Tsai * William S. Peters, Sr.

The Year of the Poet V
August 2018

Featured Poets
Hussein Habasch * Mircea Dan Duta * Naida Mujkić * Swagat Das

The Lapita

The Poetry Posse 2018

Gail Weston Shazor * Nizar Sartawi * Hülya N. Yilmaz
Jackie Davis Allen * Caroline 'Ceri' Nazareno
Alicja Maria Kubenska * Teresa E. Gallion
Kimberly Burnham * Shareef Abdur – Rasheed
Ashok K. Bhargava* Elizabeth Castillo * Swapna Behaera
Tezmin Ition Tsai * William S. Peters, Sr.

Now Available

www.innerchildpress.com/the-year-of-the-poet

The Year of the Poet V
September 2018

The Aztecs & Incas

Featured Poets
Kolade Olanrewaju Freedom
Eliza Segiet
Mazher Hussain Abdul Ghani
Lily Swarn

The Poetry Posse 2018

Gail Weston Shazor * Nizar Sartawi * Hülya N. Yılmaz
Jackie Davis Allen * Caroline 'Ceri' Nazareno
Alicja Maria Kubeska * Teresa E. Gallion
Kimberly Burnham * Shareef Abdur – Rasheed
Ashok K. Bhargava * Elizabeth Castillo * Swapna Behera
Tezmin Ition Tsai * William S. Peters, Sr.

The Year of the Poet V
October 2018

Featured Poets
Alicia Minjarez * Lonneice Weeks-Badley
Lopamudra Mishra * Abdelwahed Souayah

Bengali

The Poetry Posse 2018

Gail Weston Shazor * Nizar Sartawi * Hülya N. Yılmaz
Jackie Davis Allen * Caroline 'Ceri' Nazareno
Alicja Maria Kubeska * Teresa E. Gallion
Kimberly Burnham * Shareef Abdur – Rasheed
Ashok K. Bhargava * Elizabeth Castillo * Swapna Behera
Tezmin Ition Tsai * William S. Peters, Sr.

The Year of the Poet V
November 2018

Featured Poets
Michelle Joan Barulich * Monsif Beroual
Krystyna Konecka * Nassira Nezzar

The Poetry Posse 2018

Gail Weston Shazor * Nizar Sartawi * Hülya N. Yılmaz
Jackie Davis Allen * Caroline 'Ceri' Nazareno
Alicja Maria Kubeska * Teresa E. Gallion
Kimberly Burnham * Shareef Abdur – Rasheed
Ashok K. Bhargava * Elizabeth Castillo * Swapna Behera
Tezmin Ition Tsai * William S. Peters, Sr.

The Year of the Poet V
December 2018

Featured Poets
Rose Terranova Cirigliano
Joanna Kalinowska
Sokolović Emir
Dr. T. Ashok Chakravarthy

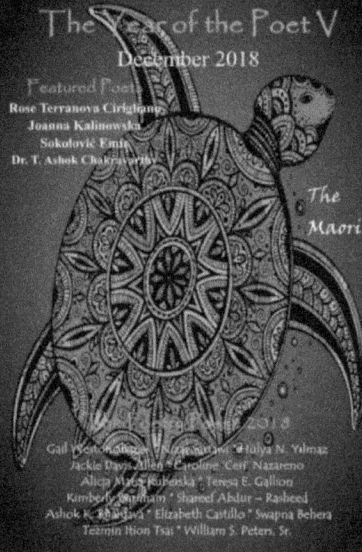

The Maori

The Poetry Posse 2018

Gail Weston Shazor * Nizar Sartawi * Hülya N. Yılmaz
Jackie Davis Allen * Caroline 'Ceri' Nazareno
Alicja Maria Kubeska * Teresa E. Gallion
Kimberly Burnham * Shareef Abdur – Rasheed
Ashok K. Bhargava * Elizabeth Castillo * Swapna Behera
Tezmin Ition Tsai * William S. Peters, Sr.

Now Available

www.innerchildpress.com/the-year-of-the-poet

The Year of the Poet VI

January 2019

Indigenous North Americans

Featured Poets

Houda Elfchtali
Anthony Briscoe
Iram Fatima 'Ashi'
Dr. K. K. Mathew

Dream Catcher

The Poetry Posse 2019

Gail Weston Shazor * Joe Paire * Hülya N. Yilmaz
Jackie Davis Allen * Caroline Gill Nazareno
Alicja Maria Kuberska * Teresa E. Gallion
Kimberly Burnham * Shareef Abdur – Rasheed
Ashok K. Bhargava * Elizabeth Castillo * Swapna Behera
Tezmin Ition Tsai * William S. Peters, Sr.

The Year of the Poet VI

February 2019

Featured Poets

Marek Lukaszewicz * Bharati Nayak
Aida G. Roque * Jean-Jacques Fournier

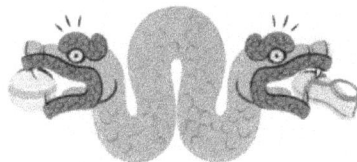

Meso-America

The Poetry Posse 2019

Gail Weston Shazor * Albert Carrasco * Hülya N. Yilmaz
Jackie Davis Allen * Caroline Nazareno * Eliza Segiet
Alicja Maria Kuberska * Teresa E. Gallion * Joe Paire
Kimberly Burnham * Shareef Abdur – Rasheed
Ashok K. Bhargava * Elizabeth Castillo * Swapna Behera
Tezmin Ition Tsai * William S. Peters, Sr.

The Year of the Poet VI

March 2019

Featured Poets

Enesa Mahmić * Sylwia K. Malinowska
Sharouk Hammoud * Anwer Ghani

The Caribbean

The Poetry Posse 2019

Gail Weston Shazor * Albert Carrasco * Hülya N. Yilmaz
Jackie Davis Allen * Caroline Nazareno * Eliza Segiet
Alicja Maria Kuberska * Teresa E. Gallion * Joe Paire
Kimberly Burnham * Shareef Abdur – Rasheed
Ashok K. Bhargava * Elizabeth Castillo * Swapna Behera
Tezmin Ition Tsai * William S. Peters, Sr.

The Year of the Poet VI

April 2019

Featured Poets

DL Davis * Michelle Joan Barulich
Lulëzim Haziri * Faleeha Hassan

Central & West Africa

The Poetry Posse 2019

Gail Weston Shazor * Albert Carrasco * Hülya N. Yilmaz
Jackie Davis Allen * Caroline Nazareno * Eliza Segiet
Alicja Maria Kuberska * Teresa E. Gallion * Joe Paire
Kimberly Burnham * Shareef Abdur – Rasheed
Ashok K. Bhargava * Elizabeth Castillo * Swapna Behera
Tezmin Ition Tsai * William S. Peters, Sr.

Now Available

www.innerchildpress.com/the-year-of-the-poet

The Year of the Poet VI
May 2019

Featured Poets
Emad Al-Haydary * Hussein Nasser Jabr
Wahab Sheriff * Abdul Razzaq Al Ameeri

Asia Southeast Asia and Maritime Asia

The Poetry Posse 2019

Gail Weston Shazor * Albert Carrasco * Hülya N. Yılmaz
Jackie Davis Allen * Caroline Nazareno * Eliza Segiet
Alicja Maria Kuberska * Teresa E. Gallion * Joe Paire
Kimberly Burnham * Shareef Abdur – Rasheed
Ashok K. Bhargava * Elizabeth Castillo * Swapna Behera
Tezmin Ition Tsai * William S. Peters, Sr.

The Year of the Poet VI
June 2019

Featured Poets
Kate Gaudi Powiekszone * Sahaj Sabharwal
Iwu Jeff * Mohamed Abdel Aziz Shmeis

Arctic
Circumpolar

The Poetry Posse 2019

Gail Weston Shazor * Albert Carrasco * Hülya N. Yılmaz
Jackie Davis Allen * Caroline Nazareno * Eliza Segiet
Alicja Maria Kuberska * Teresa E. Gallion * Joe Paire
Kimberly Burnham * Shareef Abdur – Rasheed
Ashok K. Bhargava * Elizabeth Castillo * Swapna Behera
Tezmin Ition Tsai * William S. Peters, Sr.

The Year of the Poet VI

Featured Poets
Saadeddin Shahin   Andy Scott
Fahredin Shehu   Alok Kumar Ray

The Horn of Africa

Ethiopia   Djibouti

Somalia   Eritrea

The Poetry Posse 2019

Gail Weston Shazor * Albert Carrasco * Hülya N. Yılmaz
Jackie Davis Allen * Caroline Nazareno * Eliza Segiet
Alicja Maria Kuberska * Teresa E. Gallion * Joe Paire
Kimberly Burnham * Shareef Abdur – Rasheed
Ashok K. Bhargava * Elizabeth Castillo * Swapna Behera
Tezmin Ition Tsai * William S. Peters, Sr.

The Year of the Poet VI
August 2019

Featured Poets
Shola Balogun * Bharati Nayak
Monalisa Dash Dwibedy * Mbizo Chirasha

Coexist

Southwest Asia

The Poetry Posse 2019

Gail Weston Shazor * Albert Carrasco * Hülya N. Yılmaz
Jackie Davis Allen * Caroline Nazareno * Eliza Segiet
Alicja Maria Kuberska * Teresa E. Gallion * Joe Paire
Kimberly Burnham * Shareef Abdur – Rasheed
Ashok K. Bhargava * Elizabeth Castillo * Swapna Behera
Tezmin Ition Tsai * William S. Peters, Sr.

Now Available

www.innerchildpress.com/the-year-of-the-poet

and there is much, much more !

visit . . .

www.innerchildpress.com/antho
logies-sales-special.php

Also check out our Authors and
all the wonderful Books
Available at :

www.innerchildpress.com/autho
rs-pages

INNER CHILD PRESS

WORLD HEALING WORLD PEACE
2018

A Poetry Anthology for Humanity

Now Available

www.worldhealingworldpeacepoetry.com

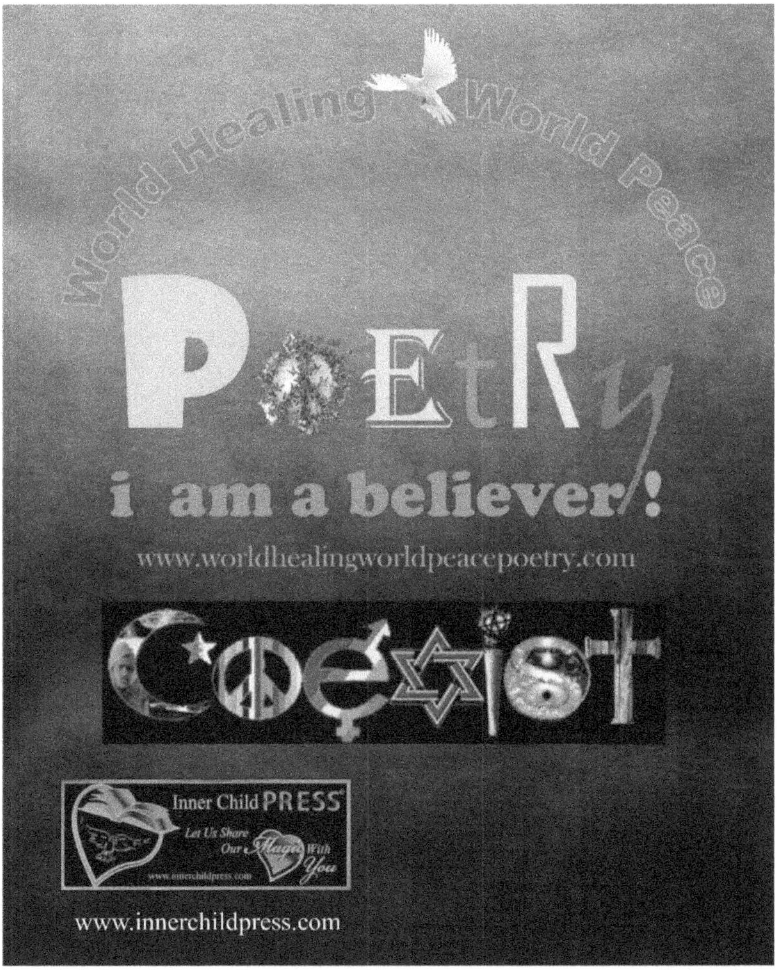

Now Available

www.worldhealingworldpeacepoetry.com

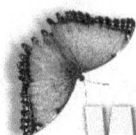

I Support

World Healing
World Peace

www.worldhealingworldpeacepoetry.com

World Healing World Peace

i am a believer !

World Healing World Peace 2018

Now Available

www.worldhealingworldpeacepoetry.com

Inner Child Press International

'building bridges of cultural understanding'

Meet the Board of Directors

William S. Peters, Sr.
Chair Person
Founder
Inner Child Enterprises
Inner Child Press

Hülya N Yılmaz
Director
Editing Services
Co-Chair Person

Fahredin B. Shehu
Director
Cultural Affairs

Elizabeth E. Castillo
Director
Recording Secretary

De'Andre Hawthorne
Director
Performance Poetry

Gail Weston Shazor
Director
Anthologies

Kimberly Burnham
Director
Cultural Ambassador
Pacific Northwest
USA

Ashok K. Bhargava
Director
WINAwards

Deborah Smart
Director
Publicity
Marketing

www.innerchildpress.com

Inner Child Press International

'building bridges of cultural understanding'

Meet our Cultural Ambassadors

Fahredin Shehu
Director of Cultural

Faleeha Hassan
Iraq – USA

Elizabeth E. Castillo
Philippines

Antoinette Coleman
Chicago
Midwest USA

Ananda Nepali
Nepal – Egypt
Southern India

Kimberly Burnham
Pacific Northwest
USA

Alicja Kuberska
Poland
Eastern Europe

Swapna Behera
India
Southeast Asia

Kolade O. Freedom
Nigeria
West Africa

Mousif Bennani
Morocco
Northern Africa

Ashok K. Bhargava
Canada

Tzemin Ition Tsai
Republic of China
Greater China

Alicia M. Ramirez
Mexico
Central America

Christena AV Williams
Jamaica
Caribbean

Louise Hudon
Eastern Canada

Aziz Mountassir
Morocco
Northern Africa

Shareef Abdur-Rasheed
Southeastern USA

Laure Charazac
France
Western Europe

Mohammad Ikbal Harb
Lebanon
Middle East

Mohamed Abdel
Aziz Shmeis
Egypt
Middle East

Hilary Mainga
Kenya
Eastern Africa

Josephus R. Johnson
Liberia

www.innerchildpress.com

201

This Anthological Publication
is underwritten solely by

Inner Child Press

Inner Child Press is a Publishing Company Founded and Operated by Writers. Our personal publishing experiences provides us an intimate understanding of the sometimes daunting challenges Writers, New and Seasoned may face in the Business of Publishing and Marketing their Creative "Written Work".

For more Information

Inner Child Press

www.innerchildpress.com

Inner Child Press International

'building bridges of cultural understanding'

202 Wiltree Court, State College, Pennsylvania 16801

www.innerchildpress.com

~ fini ~

Coming
April 2020

Inner Child Press International

The
World Healing, World Peace
International Poetry Symposium

Stay Tuned

for more information

intouch@innerchildpress.com

'building bridges of cultural understanding'

www.innerchildpress.com

www.ingramcontent.com/pod-product-compliance
Lightning Source LLC
LaVergne TN
LVHW011153080426
835508LV00007B/381